CW01582170

'Frankie Says ... ' grown-up stories about growing up in the 70s & 80s

A nostalgic trip down memory lane, via the pop culture of our youth, to a simpler world we're all far too old to remember much about.

About the author

Gavin grew up in the 70s/80s in a market town in middle England. The rest you can work out from reading the stories themselves.

About the illustrator

Rob started Posteritty in 2013 and created a new form of minimalist poster art based on popular culture. Ricky Gervais described it as 'really pretty good' and you don't get much higher praise than that. Cards, posters and commissions are available at www.posteritty.com.

Roman Bank
Publishing

These stories are based on real-life experiences. Most of the content is absolutely true. The rest is either exaggerated, made up or mis-remembered.

I would normally leave it to you to work out what falls into each category but I've been asked to point out from a legal perspective that it is safest to assume this is entirely a work of fiction, except in the case of historical fact … and I wouldn't be too sure of that either. If in doubt, please assume that the names, characters and incidents portrayed in it are the work of the author's imagination. Any resemblance to actual persons, living or dead, events or localities is entirely coincidental (ok, that's not strictly true). To be clear though, any events or persons you think you may recognise are always included with the fondest of memories and anything remotely negative or libellous is genuinely for comedic purposes only and not to be taken seriously.

Every effort has been made to obtain the necessary permissions with reference to copyrighted material, both illustrative & quoted. We apologise for any omissions in this respect and will be pleased to make the appropriate acknowledgements in any future edition.

Hardback ISBN: 978-1-3999-2878-6

Set in 11.5/15.8 Sabon Next LT: typeset by Roman Bank Publishing

First published 2022: 001

Gavin Canham and Rob Marchant assert the moral right to be identified as the author and illustrator of the work respectively … unless someone really does bring a legal case against it in which case it's all down to Roman Bank Publishing which, fortunately, is a company with (very) limited liability and full insurance.

'Various' Mix Tape photo reproduced with kind permission of David Bridgland.

'Lucky Typewriter' font used with kind permission of Lukas Krakora.

© 2022 Gavin Canham. All rights reserved. No part of this publication can be reproduced, stored in a retrieval system or transmitted in any form or by any means without the prior permission of the writer, illustrator and publisher.

Dedication

For Fleagle, Bingo, Drooper and Snork without whom Saturday mornings in the 70s wouldn't have been half as much fun.

With Thanks To:

No one. Literally no one. OK, perhaps my wife, Renée, who laughed at some of the stories (just some of them, mind) but only when she thought I wasn't watching. And as for my children, Jake & Hayley … I know most of the references meant nothing to you but surely you could've pretended to show an interest? I love you all anyway. A lot.

Rob's asked me to say thanks to Kate (and Molly & Freddie) whose support/tolerance helped him move from accountancy to making doodles for a living.

Foreword

When I was younger, growing up in the 70s & 80s, I assumed the natural order of things meant that the world was always destined to improve and, one day, my life would be free of frustration and full of wonderful experiences instead.

Things started promisingly: we got loads more TV channels, shops opened on Sunday that you actually wanted to visit and phones were invented which could store your entire record collection in your pocket.

But then it all began to go pear-shaped and I now yearn for the simplicity of my childhood when speech was free (unless you were a member of Sinn Fein being interviewed by Robin Day), fake news was something you watched on the Two Ronnies and what you wanted to be when you grew up was a job not a gender.

So, I had a choice: either spend a small fortune on eBay buying up over-priced nostalgia or write some stories about the experiences we all shared back then. I ended up writing a story a week on the Frankie Says website for 50 weeks at www.absoluteveryfirsttime.com (now www.frankie-says.co.uk too). Obviously, I bought a shitload of memorabilia off eBay as well.

The stories are mostly true but I threw in a few blatant lies which I tended to think were pretty obvious but clearly, as it turned out, not to everyone (one Facebook user asked me for proof that Phil Collins had actually dipped his hand into the pot destined for the Ethiopians during Live Aid).

Rob is responsible for the fantastic illustrations which transport our character, Frankie, back to the great pop culture moments of the 70s & 80s ... and, yes, both of us know that the phrase was created for Frankie Goes to Hollywood in 1984 by Paul Morley and so is often used by us anachronistically and we also know that it was originally 'Frankie Say' but, as we told another helpful FB user, we used a bit of artistic licence and naively didn't think it would bother anyone.

So, we hope you enjoy these trips down memory lane. Please don't take them too seriously and, if there's anything which offends you, try not to start a social media campaign to cancel us. Just let it go and smile instead about people & places we all remember from a time when life was far simpler and possibly, for the most part, a little kinder too.

G.C.

Chapters

1 MIX TAPES

The absolute very first time I made a mix tape was in 1979 when I recorded my friend Rachel playing an Atari game (badly) and then decided to add what I felt sure were some of her favourite tunes to the cassette so I could present it to her as a gift. I've still got the tape so either 1) I liked the songs so much I decided not to give it to her or 2) she didn't like the songs very much and decided to give it back. She went out with me for a week and chucked me on my fifteenth birthday so you'll guess which one my money's on.

Nowadays, it's the press of a button on Spotify but, in the 70s/80s, compiling a 90 minute mix tape was an exercise of pyramid-building proportions. Most of the songs needed to be taped off the radio – which is why so many of my mix tapes have Peter Powell or the Hairy Cornflake (never trust a man who makes up his own nickname) ruining the tracks by talking over them – or off Top of the Pops by holding your tape recorder close to the Radio Rentals TV screen and trying to avoid static shock.

Creating a mix tape was an art which required patience, skill and practice. You'd sit for hours in front of the radio or TV, fingers poised over the play & record buttons, waiting for any song you vaguely liked to be aired. The process was littered with potential pitfalls: false alarms when the opening bars of what you thought was the Clash turned out to be Cliff Richard, cock-ups when your chubby fingers only managed to press one of the record buttons and the inevitable end-of-tape fiasco when you needed to flip the cartridge over mid-tune to start recording on the other side. This was an exercise which required such high levels of dexterity and co-ordination that Formula One racing teams should've made it a mandatory requirement for the recruitment of their pit-stop engineers.

And, once you'd sacrificed several weekends putting 90 minutes of music together, there was a fair chance that your sony walkman would chew it up and render it useless anyway. Several of my mix tapes have sections of sellotape where I had to cut out a mangled piece of tape and splice the remaining ends together. That tended to have a rather truncated effect on the songs and made lip-synching to them in front of the mirror a frustrating process – one moment you were a dandy highwayman who people were too scared to mention and the next you were da diddly qua qua.

The Top 40 countdown on Radio One every Sunday evening was a great source of mix tape tracks, presented in my time by Simon Bates on top of his week-day morning show. I may be the only one to think that guessing the year in the 'Golden Hour' at 10:00 was a far superior entertainment slot than 'Our Tune' at 11:00 but I suppose that explains my complete lack of empathy (I'm a bloke after all) as well as the rather unhealthy obsession I have with quiz shows like Blockbusters (in which, incidentally, a boy in the year above me at school was the first to ask Bob Holness if he could have a 'P' and a nation duly split its sides).

Apart from Batesy, the other recognisable voices on my tapes belong to Tony Blackburn and Tommy Vance whose inane comments, recorded of course over the best parts of the songs, prove just how much Harry Enfield and Paul Whitehouse toned down the caricatures for Smashie & Nicey.

There is no sign of Mike Read on tape (no, not the Eastenders bloke who presented Runaround on TV and encouraged playgrounds nationwide to kick off their games of British Bulldog with shouts of "g-g-g-g-g-go" ... at least while local authorities allowed us to play it) but I guess he was too busy climbing onto his high horse and ensuring that Frankie Goes to Hollywood were banned from the radio for telling us to relax when we wanted to come. I'm not sure if he ever turned his attention to school playground games but I wouldn't rule him out as the one who got British Bulldog banned either.

I've got about 30 of these tapes up in the attic (that's a solid 18 months of sweat and toil) and three of them can still be played in full without the sellotape clogging up the machinery. It's so refreshing to listen to a playlist which has been generated by loving patience rather than algorithms. And how enjoyable is it to run through a compilation of songs which, with the exception of my John Peel show recordings, are unbounded by limits of genre or style and united only by a moment in time (probably, I accept, because a few of them were recorded by mistake)? "Very" is the answer to that rather convoluted question.

Oh, and there's always the chance you'll get to hear priceless snippets of sanctimonious and self-important bullshit from disc jockeys like Peter

Powell. On one of my tapes, he jumps onto Mike Read's high horse to lecture Madness over their choice of 'cardiac arrest' as the theme of their new single before going on to play 'I want candy' by Bow Wow Wow (their lead singer still some months short of her 16th birthday) and proving himself the only person in the country who actually believed it was a song about sweets.

When I published the story originally, an old friend of mine from college posted this photo on the website (along with some technical nerdy stuff about Dual 505 turntables and Akai cassette decks – I lost interest at that point to be honest). I love so much about it:

1. *It's wonderfully eclectic (the Ruts, AC/DC and Judie Tzuke!!)*
2. *It's so neatly written (even the lightning sign between AC and DC)*
3. *He spelt Masquerade wrong…but he was an engineer so, to be fair, I'm surprised he spelt the rest of the playlist right*
4. *I love the title – I called all of my tapes 'VARIOUS' too!*

2 SUMMER HOLIDAYS

The absolute very first time I remember going on holiday was to North Devon in the late 60s or early 70s. In fact, it could easily have been the late 70s or early 80s instead for that matter because we went to the same place every year. Everyone did in those days. One summer we went to the next bay along for a change but Mum & Dad felt that was quite enough excitement for their lifetime so we reverted back to our usual place the following year.

Compared to our kids, we weren't used to choice when we were growing up. Viewing entertainment was three TV channels not several hundred and nothing was 'on demand' – you were just grateful to get a half-decent signal from your TV aerial which, if you had a portable telly, sat on top of your set and you wiggled it until the picture finally appeared, usually just as the end credits for your programme started to roll. There were no cinema multiplexes so, if you wanted to see an action film at the pictures and they were showing Love Story, that's what you watched. There weren't 25 different varieties of coffee and tea in our day either. Arabica beans were what posh people had with their Sunday roast and elderflower & thistle were things you tried your hardest to avoid treading on during a walk. We got what we were offered. That's it.

We never flew anywhere on holiday (though we heard that the jet-set took flights to somewhere called Torremolinos which sounded very exotic). Instead, we loaded up the car (this was a time when family cars were normal-sized and would probably fit in the boot of one of today's MPVs) by hauling our suitcases onto the roof rack and hoping they'd stay in place with a bit of tarpaulin and some bungee cords which Dad would nick off my bike and forget to put back afterwards, ensuring my satchel flew off the next time I rode to school and ended up being run over by a Morris Marina.

Heading off on hols, there was no Sat Nav so we used something called a map (and not a google one that talked to you from the palm of your hand) which invariably led to the family-favourite car game of guessing who was to blame when we got lost or took a wrong turn. It was always Dad's fault even though mum had the map and to suggest otherwise from the back seat meant missing a turn the next time the tin of boiled sweets was handed round.

With the only other light relief coming from announcing in unison the moment we crossed from one county into another (we're in Shiteshire ... NOW), car journeys were hell for kids in the 70s. There were no commercial radio stations which played songs from the Hit Parade so we had to listen to one of the BBC options and, in those days, parents tended not to be hip enough to tune into Radio One so instead we got Jimmy Young (who, as far as we could tell, rarely lived up to his name). Nowadays, kids stream Elton John on their AirPods while their parents throw some shapes to the latest Dua Lipa track from the Spotify playlist they've paired with the car stereo.

There were no gadgets or mobile phones to keep us occupied (the Rubiks cube didn't count) so we played I-Spy. For hours. If we tried to read or draw something, one of us would be sick. My mum put a yellow potty in the back of the car just for this eventuality. Unfortunately, it was the same yellow potty which all three of us had learned on as toddlers (back then, being potty-trained involved an actual potty) and that fact alone would make us feel far sicker than the car journey ever did. Between toilet breaks, sick stops and hunting for whichever petrol station offered the holographic wildlife cards or football coins I was collecting, any journey to go on holiday took nearly as long as the holiday itself. No wonder we kept on asking whether we were there yet.

Once we got to the hotel, we'd head straight to the beach regardless of the weather (yes, it used to rain a bit back then but I remember our summer holidays as always sunny even if they weren't). We didn't have Factor 50 in those days – our version was Factor 0 and useless – so we'd stay out all day and were burnt to a crisp by the time we got back to the hotel in the evening. Luckily, there was no such thing as skin cancer then either although we'd heard enough about our kitchen appliances causing a hole in something called the Ozone layer that our mum would give us a slap whenever we left the fridge door open for any length of time.

Days on the beach were always fun with lessons in domestic violence followed by a dose of animal cruelty. Dad would take us to watch a Punch & Judy show where the bloke would slap the woman over the head with a truncheon and tell the assembled fathers "that's the way to do it". We'd then be plonked on top of some malnourished and over-worked donkey to be ridden around in small circles for a couple of minutes while it crapped in the sand behind us. It wasn't exactly the Grand National.

After that, we'd stage games of cricket where Dad would invite nearby families to participate in the hope that he'd have someone to go to the pub with later. My sister was supposed to be wicketkeeper but tended to go crabbing in one of the rockpools instead (which, for the avoidance of doubt, was fishing for crabs with a small net).

We'd take so much kit down to the beach it was as though we were on a jungle expedition. Nowadays, people saunter down with a small backpack and, within minutes, have managed to assemble four chairs, a table, a couple of paddle boards with built-in lycra wetsuits and a gazebo with running fresh hot water. In our day, it would take all morning to hammer in our moth-eaten windbreak while making several trips to the car to fetch some rusty deckchairs, the cricket bat & stumps and a couple of wooden surfboards which tended not to float very well. We didn't need the wetsuits though. Hard as nails in those days.

There was always a child-hating sod who drove the ice cream van, turning on his musical jingle only at the last minute and then accelerating away as soon as we started racing towards him with enough cash for a 99 or strawberry mivvi. No wonder child obesity was a rarity in our day. If we weren't chasing ice cream vans or running after cricket balls hit miles away by competitive dads, we were haring along the beach with a kite you could hold in one hand rather than one which required a harness or towed you out to sea.

And before we left to go home, we'd be forced to write postcards which would arrive at their destination several days after we did. This was an exercise on par with Xmas card-writing and took up most of the final day. The postcards tended to be poorly-printed aerial photos of our beach where we would mark our position with a biroed X but Dad would also get some of the saucy seaside ones to send to his mates (usually well-endowed women complaining that their ageing husbands got a little stiff in the mornings – the cards, that is, not his mates).

We only used to have one holiday a year and it was in the UK – we didn't get to enjoy several short Euro breaks, a skiing trip, a safari and a fund-raiser to save the turtles in Costa Rica – so leaving would always be a time for sadness ... not least because we knew we had Jimmy Young, yellow potties and polyester seats chafing the backs of our sun-burned legs to look forward to on the way home. Salad days.

I've just found this old photo which shows exactly how we travelled on holiday in the old days. You might think this is a personalised nameplate but they had it before I was born so I honestly think that's where they got the idea for my name from.

3 SHOPS NO LONGER ON THE HIGH ST

I can't remember the absolute very first time I realised that one of our high street shops had closed down but I recall the shock when I came back home after college in the mid 80s and there was a bingo hall instead of the old cinema in Broad St. The owners had seen the writing on the wall when Blockbuster Video came along but little did they know who'd end up having the last laugh in that particular tussle.

We'd also allowed the local brewery (which sold barrels direct to punters) to stop brewing beer and turn into a museum (which didn't). It was then I made the decision to move to London once my studies were over. They still had plenty of cinemas and breweries down there but, as I later found out, muggings, burglaries and bomb scares too. My own town may have lost some of its entertainment options but it was hardly a hotbed of crime or, as far as I knew, on the IRA hitlist either.

I guess the first major shop closure I remember in our town was probably Freeman Hardy & Willis once people realised that buying sensible shoes from a retail outlet which sounded like a firm of accountants wasn't something you'd want to brag about to your friends.

We had so many greengrocers, butchers, laundrettes and jewellers that we'd never go hungry, dirty or deprived of crap bracelets (Gerald Ratner teaching us that, even before smartphones & social media, unguarded comments could still 'go viral' and come back to haunt you). However, in my home town at least, we had nowhere to buy clothes (except Fosters which clearly didn't count). There weren't even any charity shops back then where you could cobble together an outfit and try to pass it off as fashion. I lived off hand-me-downs instead but my brother was so much older than me that, as a teenager, I ended up looking like a hippy which was not a good look in the early 80s ... or any other time.

There were plenty of places to rent TVs though – either at Rumbelows or Radio Rentals (where you didn't actually rent radios so sack the brand agency) – or buy pipe tobacco (which kept my Dad happy and helped my passive smoking habit) or book holidays abroad at Thomas Cook or Lunn Poly because the other option was ringing up the hotels yourself which tended to cost you as much as the holiday in those days.

There were two shops which were in almost every High St in the land, one of which has amazingly survived to this day. WH Smiths somehow continues to fend off far superior on-line competitors despite the fact that everything it sells can be bought more cheaply and with far more enjoyment off the internet. It's probably like the Crystal Maze or modern Escape Rooms – there's a real sense of achievement when you emerge, relatively unscathed, clutching an over-priced CD which you could listen to for free on Spotify or a £5 book which would cost 11p on Amazon and get delivered by the time you'd made it back home from town.

The second shop, obviously, was Woolies. Ours was housed in an historic building (a perfect fit with cheap records and pick 'n' mix) on the site of an ex-butchers. I read in an old newspaper cutting that a cow had fallen in front of this butcher's pony trap in the first half of the 1900s – I've no idea from how high – and he wasn't the same since so sold to FW Woolworth & Sons in the 50s. I'm honestly not making that up.

It's easy (and incredibly tempting) to make fun of Woolies but it was the perfect place to search out the latest singles without getting drawn into some existential debate by the old farts who ran the local independent record shop. I know it's incredible nowadays to have every song you've ever heard/liked/owned in the palm of your hand but there was really something special about poring over the cover of an album before setting down the needle and hearing those clicks and scratches as the song started. Anyway, back to Woolies … is an idea which didn't occur to anywhere near enough people in 2008 to prevent the chain from closing.

The local newspaper had its office slapbang on the High St instead of the back room of someone's flat with a printer, mobile phone and google. We had banks before they became trendy wine bars or coffee shops (what we wouldn't have given for that innovation to come earlier – although there were no cashpoints or credit cards in those days so, without banks, we'd have struggled to pay for a latte even if we knew what one of them was) and we had Timothy Whites before they were given the Boots (bad pun – that's who took them over).

There may not have been coffee shop chains but there were still plenty of places where schoolkids could gather around a hot drink and make it last for a good couple of hours before getting kicked out. Our local Wimpy was a particular favourite because it had Missile Command and Knickerbocker Glory. Just to be clear, only one of those was actually on the menu. We fed 10p pieces into the other one. Lots of them. I feel a little hypocritical accusing my game-playing kids of being anti-social but, don't worry, I'd never admit that to them.

I don't think Snappy Snaps ever came to our town so we either had to post our film off to Truprint or get it developed at Boots where, when you picked up the photos, you just KNEW the spotty-faced twat behind the counter had taken a good look through each of them and probably printed duplicates of the one of your mum in her bikini on Woolacombe beach.

The advent of mobile phones (yes, kids, they didn't exist when we were your age and yet we still survived) did for the film developers just as the ability to print posters at home to plaster over your bedroom wall made Athena (and probably Smash Hits) obsolete. And the owners of Tie Rack, already nervous of the change in office dress code policy, must've known they were completely buggered when even lawyers and estate agents started to loosen their top button.

Besides these chains, the rest of the High St was either independents or pubs, both of which had limited opening hours in our day (unless you happened to be friendly with one of the landlord's daughters in which case St Marys Vaults was yours to enjoy outside opening hours to your heart's content … and there's nothing more likely to cure a fruit machine addiction, I can assure you, than playing one for free until five o'clock in the morning).

Our toy shop was a magical treasure trove where you could while away hours pretending to be Tom Hanks off Big (even though he wasn't much older than us at the time so was yet to take up the role) and I'd even travel to London (it took about a day or so back then) to visit a comic shop called 'Dark They Were And Golden-Eyed' which deserved to survive for the name alone.

It's ironic that these types of interesting, quirky and innovative shops have all but disappeared, to be replaced by bland chains and 'copy & paste' outlets, at the very time when the High St needs to be interesting, quirky and innovative to take on the faceless on-line giants. Store owners and assistants who knew their products and could genuinely help you choose what suited you best have been phased out by call centres and self-service check-outs just when customer service would be the best competitive advantage against internet shopping.

Bring back the quirky shops. Re-hire the knowledgeable staff who not only knew their merchandise inside out but knew you, your family and your domestic pets equally as well. Bring back Freeman Hardy & Willis. What was that? I've gone too far haven't I?

4 A TRIP TO THE CINEMA

The absolute very first time I went to the cinema with a girl was to see Abba The Movie in 1977 in my final year at Primary School. This, as I've recently googled, was the year before the film actually hit the British cinema screens but I'm going to stick with it if you don't mind because everything else I remember ties in with it being 1977 and whatever fragile confidence I have left in my mental well-being will disappear otherwise (although nowadays that will probably get me an outpouring of sympathy in the office and a large pay rise instead of the stifled giggles and L for Loooo-ser signs I'd have got from my workmates in the past).

It was just over a year after the Sex Pistols played their first gig but I grew up in a market town in Lincolnshire pre-internet so news took a while to reach us – usually 18 months or so – which meant my nascent 11 year old class warrior-self was still slightly more super-trooper than anti-christ or anarchist.

I went on an official date to the cinema with Miranda. This was a little uncomfortable for me because my girlfriend at the time was Sarah but we had never been on a date together and she wasn't fully aware of being my girlfriend so that helped ease my conscience to some degree. Outside of class, the only time I actually saw Sarah, and sometimes said hello, was from an adjacent pew in the Sunday church service which we attended with our respective families. I rarely got an acknowledgement – perhaps a half-smile as she knelt in prayer (presumably for a divine restraining order) – and yet she was the only reason I agreed to skip Captain Scarlet and The Mysterons on a Sunday morning in the first place. I strongly suspect that my fierce atheism in later life was a direct consequence of the misery I felt from her rejection ... so, not an entirely wasted journey after all.

Miranda, on the other hand, was not much of a church-goer. She'd turned up in our final year at St Gilbert of Sempringham's school and, compared to me and my young chums, was clearly 'mature for her age.' She gave me my first proper kiss when my arm was in a sling from a sprained wrist (a football accident ... honest) so I was hardly in a position to hold her off. I'm assuming it was this deviant behaviour which had led to her departure from her previous school(s). St Gilberts prided itself on its inclusivity though – frankly they'd let anyone in – so Miranda got to finish her primary education in a school rather than a correctional institution.

I don't have many comparisons but I think it was a pretty normal co-ed place. Break-times were a blur of activity with games of British Bulldog and Kiss-Chase. I tried to target Sarah in both of them and I was no slouch but, boy, could she run fast when she needed to. Otherwise there were huddles of small groups dotted around the playground, swapping tea cards, playing paper fortune teller or watching Michelle's little sister show you her knickers if you gave her a fruit salad. Every now and then, someone would sneak off to write 'Yorkie is a bender' in the boys toilets but, largely, it was a happy place for everyone. Well, except Yorkie I guess.

If 1978 really was the date Abba The Movie was released, Miranda and I had both managed to escape the clutches of St Gilbert's by the time we'd stood in the queue for the cinema and handed over some small change for those little pink ticket stubs. My mum had told me to buy a present for my date but my suggestion of a bag of cola bottles and a few shrimps didn't seem to meet with her approval so she gave me a small bottle of anais anais which was not only a fancy new perfume but one that mum clearly didn't like as much as dad thought she would.

I'm not sure if it was my hilarious Mork & Mindy "nanu nanu" impression or the little gift-wrapped bottle I slipped into her hand as we made our way across the foyer but Miranda immediately steered us to the back of the stalls, despite us having perfectly good seats nearer the front, and made it clear that this might be my first date but it certainly wasn't hers.

Humming along to S.O.S. clearly made no difference to her. In fact my high-pitched treble, soon to grace the choir stalls of All Saints Church for two poorly-paid and deeply-troubling years, only appeared to spur her on. Fortunately, my sprained wrist had healed by then and was out of its sling so I was more capable of fending her off this time, allowing me to spend future Sundays in church trying to catch Sarah's eye with no hint of guilt but, sadly, not much success either.

I went to the cinema again recently for the first time in ages and noticed several changes (I'm very observant). Pearl & Dean weren't in charge of the advertising anymore and people gave me funny looks, for some reason, when I loudly hummed Papa Papa Papa Papa Papapa, Papa Papa

Papaaaaa PA. You didn't get your ticket from someone who looked like a bus conductor with a mini one-armed bandit. In fact, you didn't get a ticket at all. It was some virtual thing on your mobile phone which was just as well because you needed it to light the way to your seat (more a flatbed than a chair) since the ushers, at least when I visited our local cinema, seemed to have forgotten their torches. There were no boxes of Rowntrees Fruit Pastilles or cartons of Kia Ora and they'd replaced the ashtrays in the arm rests with drinks holders in which you were supposed to place large buckets of ice cubes with a dribble of cola at the bottom.

I went with my wife – it was a superhero movie and I know how much she likes them – but, despite the flatbed and my rather sexy Mork impression, she showed more Swedish sang-froid (yes, I know it's French) than Agnetha from Abba and managed to resist my charms for the entire film while the underage kids around us showed me exactly what my 11 year-old self had been missing all those years before.

Me at 11 with Miranda - my arm is genuinely in a sling (I've got other photos in the series to prove it but she wasn't kissing me in any of those so I didn't use them). For the avoidance of doubt (and by 'doubt' I mean 'legal repercussions'), I don't believe she was expelled for lewd behaviour. It was probably for nicking stuff instead. I don't know why the photo is orange - it's not a filter to disguise her identity (I wouldn't know how to apply it even if I wanted to). By the way, this pained expression is the face I pull for selfies nowadays too.

5 SPACE DUST & OTHER SWEETS

The absolute very first time I ate a packet of space dust was in the mid 1970s when I was still at primary school. We'd been through a phase of filling up our break-times with games of 'human weebles' but, frankly, we'd got a bit bored of it because no one seemed to get knocked over no matter how hard we pushed them so space dust came as a welcome relief.

Unlike our kids, we were so much less advertising savvy in those days. We were told that weebles wobbled but didn't fall down and, instead of the nation's youth replying loudly and in unison, "so fucking what, they're just eggs", we lapped it up and nagged our parents to empty their pockets at the nearest toy shop.

It was the same with space dust. Their Marketing Department planted numerous stories of kids sprinkling it on cat bowls or into grandma's open mouth as she slept in her chair and, for a short while, it took over from Jeremy Thorpe in the News of the World as the biggest threat to young people in British society. It was labelled a deadly choking hazard for small children but, to be honest, the only lives in danger appeared to belong to domestic pets or elderly relatives, especially if they happened to be asleep at the time.

Apparently, space dust consisted of small bubbles of carbon dioxide which produced the popping sensation and crackling noise. That doesn't sound like the healthiest of things to put in a child's mouth but it was the 1970s so there were probably worse options. I bought a modern version of the product from Amazon by accident the other day ('Fizzwhizz' – I thought it was something else) but couldn't get either of my cats to eat it which was annoying because I had the phone primed to film them and a video poised to go viral, something which, as an over-50, I naturally assume all videos can do … but just don't understand how.

I don't know if the formula's changed but the pack I bought had an ingredients list of 'SUGAR, LACTOSE, GLUCOSE, ARTIFICIAL FLAVOURING, CARBON DIOXIDE E-290'. Conscious that this might not strike the right chord with modern parents concerned over their children's diets, Marketing had added the words 'NO COLOURING USED' as though that would catapult the product into the 5-a-day category. Sorry, guys, that might have worked 40 years ago but we're wise to your game now.

Back then, my other sugar confectionery staples were fruit salads, blackjacks and sherbet dib dabs (I now gather these were actually called 'dip dabs' which I guess makes more sense as a set of instructions but loses some of the rhythmical beauty). All had their downsides; fruit salads were unnaturally day-glo and, at four for a penny, were an inexpensive route towards dental decay and blackjacks were similar but with the added bonus of staining your teeth (as well as your mouth and lips) before rotting them. Sherbet dib dabs, and I've got to be honest here, were a bit of a faff. The only thing going for them was that you could pretend you were taking cocaine ... though that was both painful and a criminal waste of dib dab.

I ought to give a quick shout-out to spangles which the Great British public voted in 2008 as the sweets they most wanted to see brought back. They came in fizzy cola, lemonade and, for some reason, 'Old English' flavours, the last of which I vaguely remember being apple and almost inedible but I might be getting mixed up with Trebor Blobs which had weird flavours like cider and strawberries & cream. Actually, the Great British public, back in 2008, may well have been getting mixed up with Blobs too – they deserve to make a comeback just for the name.

Sweet shops in the 70s seemed to operate differently from other retail outlets. I swear that in those days it was generally acceptable to wander around a corner store reading one of the comics you were possibly going to buy at the same time as eating the odd shrimp or cola bottle that you definitely weren't. Or was that just me? I have this vague memory of a kindly old lady behind the counter, happy to let the youngsters enjoy a few free treats because we reminded her of her own grandchildren. Clearly, I might have it wrong and it was actually a grumpy old bastard who'd phone up the police if we so much as glanced at a curly wurly and would have a panda car screeching to a halt outside the shop just minutes after we'd sauntered out.

My secondary school sweet of choice was Orange Tic Tacs. I would ignore the pleas from the adverts to use the lid to flick them into my mouth because I preferred to eat them straightaway rather than brush the dust and droppings off them once they'd landed on the floor. The idea from the advert was that it made you look cool but I was listening to Adam and the Ants at the time so had NO worries in that regard at all. In fact, I'd worked out that, if I didn't wash my hair for a week and then popped a hairnet over the back of it at night, my fuzzy fringe made me look a little like the dandy highwayman himself. Add a streak of Sherbet dib dabs to the bridge of my nose and across my rosy cheeks and the transformation was complete.

Adam told us that ant music was for sex people though I don't think he'd taken a good look at the kids in my school who were listening to his records. The closest they came to being sex people was sniggering about things that wobbled but didn't fall down. As for me, I was 14 years old with greasy hair, stained black teeth and powder dribbling from my nostrils. I went to church on a Sunday and was renowned for my highly-accurate Mork & Mindy impression. On top of that, I was also officially a sex person. So how on earth was I still a virgin? Sometimes, you don't always get what you deserve.

Me, Mozza, JM and the other 2

6 THE SMITHS

The absolute very first time I saw The Smiths play live was on February 16th 1984 at Leicester University. I wasn't at the University, I was still at school (and not one in Leicester either), but I'd figured that the Smiths were unlikely to turn up at the Darby & Joan Hall in my home town although I wouldn't be surprised if the Darby & Joan Hall hadn't even tried to contact them (who runs these places ... old farts? What was that? Ok, makes sense). As a result, music fans had little choice but to traipse over to Leicester whether we liked it or not (and, along with most of the people who lived there at the time, we didn't). I've heard it's a lovely place now though.

The Smiths had only released their first single late the previous year but it had caught my attention because they sang about the sun shining out of their behinds which not many bands tended to do back then. I had been searching for a new 'favourite band' and it looked like being a toss-up between Big Country and Kajagoogoo until Morrissey & the boys turned up so, if I'm ever asked what I would be if I wasn't a Smiths fan, I can safely give the same answer as Peter Crouch when he was asked what he'd be if he wasn't a footballer (google it).

I borrowed my mum's red mini to take some mates to the gig (though I probably called it a concert at the time). This was a tricky negotiation because it had only just been repaired from a trip to the same venue a couple of weeks earlier. I'd managed to crash it on the way back along the winding country lanes by taking one of the bends a little too fast. My girlfriend, Julie, had been in the car with me and so I drove unnecessarily fast to impress her, proving beyond a shadow of a doubt that, contrary to what I've been told several times since, I have always had a natural gift for understanding women.

There's a good chance I also thought my mum's little red mini had a headlamp bar & go-faster stripes and I was in fact one of the getaway drivers in the Italian Job. I know it sounds sad to copy motor racers off the telly but just take to the road on a Sunday evening after the F1 Grand Prix has been on and you'll know that I'm not the only one.

I hit a tree head-on although Julie (sensibly strapped into the passenger seat less than 12 months after seatbelts had been made compulsory – one of the few things to thank Jimmy Savile for) suggested afterwards that I managed to swerve to the right just before impact in an act of self-preservation bordering on manslaughter. She tried to tell me recently (she was the one to break up with me but, after 30 years, I magnanimously agreed to let bygones be bygones and speak to her again) that she had no recollection of the crash at all. Or of going out with me. She's even reinstated the restraining order.

This time round I managed an accident-free journey to the venue, despite the threat of snow showers, and we'd got in early enough to use the supporting band's set (the Red Guitars – very good but surprisingly poorly-named with hardly a red one in sight) to manoeuvre ourselves close to the front of the stage. We didn't have YouTube in those days but I recognised Morrissey from Top of the Pops a couple of months earlier when This Charming Man hit the heady heights of No.25 in the charts. Clearly this appearance captivated me far more than the general music-loving public because, after their virtuoso performance, the single promptly fell back down the charts the following week.

I had also been struck by the Smiths vinyl covers, especially the first single which showed a bloke's naked bum on the artwork. I know naked bums are two-a-penny nowadays but they were quite the rarity on record sleeves in 1983. I spent the first half of the gig trying to figure out whether it was Morrissey's bum on the artwork. Apparently, as I found out much later, it belonged to a chap called George. Morrissey's jeans fell straight from his waist to the back of his knees, uninterrupted by a pair of buttocks, so George's bulbous cheeks had obviously won the day.

After a handful of songs, the gig was warming up nicely. Morrissey had thrown his bunch of gladioli (my teenage daughter just asked if this was a type of pasta – I'm honestly not kidding) into the audience and the Smiths virgins amongst us (me included) thought he might not have meant to do it so we helpfully lobbed them back, most of them landing on the stage but one rogue missile hitting Johnny Marr's guitar and lodging in the fret alongside his fag.

The only musical instrument I played at that age was the recorder (not very 'indie pop' but it was compulsory at my school) and I'd rarely had anything thrown at me mid-tune so was in no position to judge my future guitar hero's reaction … which was to point his plectrum at us, throw a hissy fit and storm off stage. This seemed a little rich given the earlier flower-hurling antics of his own front-man but I think we were all quite keen to get out of Leicester before we were snowed in so we happily shuffled out of the concert hall and made our way home. I've heard it's a lovely place now though.

In hindsight, I realise that JM hadn't cut the gig short but that 45 mins was the Smiths version of a 90 mins set, an approach mirrored in their 12 inch singles where, unlike the usual remixes, live recordings and bonus tracks which other bands offered, the A-Side of a Smiths 12 inch single was remarkably similar to the A-Side of the 7 inch version. If you were lucky, the B-Side carried an extra track – usually from an album you already owned – and, for that, you had to fork out £1.99 which was twice as much as the 7 inch, nearly as much as an LP and roughly £300 in today's money. Many people would've been put off purchasing them but, with a shrewd eye on their future investment potential, I used up all my weekly wages (most schoolkids had jobs in those days – we were practically independent by the time we were 16) and bought every one I could get my hands on.

As an aside, isn't it odd that our kids don't really understand what it means to be a scratched record (and, no, not because I never drone on about the same thing over and over again – just read on to the end of the book to clear that one up)? How many of them have actually experienced a scratched record or, even better, would know to tape a halfpenny to the stylus to weigh it down and stop it jumping (anything more than a penny would damage the vinyl and, if it was a Smiths single, that could end up knocking thousands off its investment value)?

As I write this, I'm halfway through my second bottle of pinot noir and I have just paused my nightly eBay search for 80s nostalgia (Battling Tops, Fighting Furies and Subbuteo this time) so I could check on my Smiths vinyl nest egg. There are literally thousands of the bloody things on eBay at roughly the same price now as I paid in the 1980s … and they're not even scratched!! What a bummer (the George version not Morrissey's pathetic effort). I was happy in the haze of a drunken hour but heaven knows I'm miserable now (ba-dum tish).

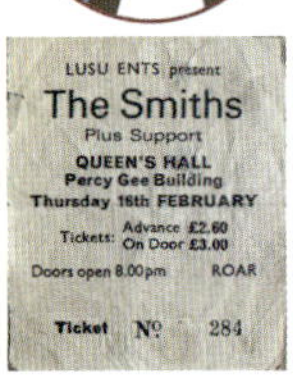
LUSU ENTS present
The Smiths
Plus Support
QUEEN'S HALL
Percy Gee Building
Thursday 16th FEBRUARY
Tickets: Advance £2.60 On Door £3.00
Doors open 8.00pm ROAR
Ticket No. 284

My ticket to the gig and one of the later Smiths albums signed by Mozza which the seller on eBay assured me was genuine despite me smudging the writing (above the i) when it turned up because the ink was still wet. He said it's typical of fountain pens in the 80s (except he sounded like a teenager so I'm not sure how he would know) and that I should keep it in a cool dark place. My wife says that means my man-cave … except for the 'cool' part.

7 SATURDAY MORNING TV

The absolute very first time I remember watching Saturday morning TV was the classic mid-1970s line-up of Champion The Wonder Horse, Wacky Races, Banana Splits and Multi-Coloured Swap Shop. Tiswas was on ITV and so was banned in my middle class house although I'd sneakily switch channels whenever John Craven was on Swap Shop (although only after I'd clocked his latest jumper so I could join in the piss-take at school on Monday).

I know that probably wasn't the actual line-up (someone is bound to google it) but it's pretty representative because both of the TV channels had a very formulaic approach to Saturday morning TV (there was a third channel – BBC2 – but no one under the age of 45 watched that except at 9pm when Monty Python, Not The Nine O'Clock News or the Young Ones were on).

In those days, apart from John Craven (if not his jumpers), silliness and juvenile humour were the main tactics in capturing the youth market at the start of the weekend. I can only assume the Beeb were contractually obliged to kick off with a live-action animal show because we always had to endure a series of potential pet-food candidates – Champion the Wonder Horse / Skippy / Lassie – before the fun began. It seems odd to say that super-smart animals solving crimes represented the least silly programme of the whole morning but they were still essential viewing compared to whatever was on BBC2 (probably Open University or the Test Card).

With Black Beauty on ITV (can a theme tune be onomatopoeic – it just sounds like a galloping horse, doesn't it? Google it and tell me I'm wrong), the only British offering in this genre on BBC was Animal Magic with Johnny Morris but by that stage, unfortunately for Johnny, the Americans had made us believe that animals really could outwit the local constabulary and rescue missing persons so putting on dodgy impressions and pretending to hold conversations with the residents of Bristol Zoo wasn't going to impress us one bit.

After that, it was cartoon heaven (I'm thinking Wacky Races, Hong Kong Phooey, Flintstones, Scooby Doo, Top Cat etc – all the Looney Tunes stable was on ITV and so was out-of-bounds for me). This was 100% American fare because British cartoons weren't invented until the 90s (apart from Mr Benn and Bod who looked like they'd been animated by kids several years below me in primary school). Instead, the Brits created cuddly puppets for a younger age group (Bagpuss, The Clangers, Basil Brush and The Wombles) but these tended to offer a serious moral message and so weren't considered silly enough for Saturday mornings.

Our friends across the Atlantic also sent us Banana Splits and the Monkees, one of which was about a band which dressed up in silly costumes and couldn't play their instruments and the other was Banan… yes, fair enough, bit of an obvious set-up and a cheap shot too (particularly because I had a schoolboy crush on Davy Jones). I've got a punk version of the Tra-La-La song by the Dickies who, while other punk bands were goading us to smash the system, preferred to reaffirm their anarchic principles by singing 'flipping like a pancake, popping like a cork, Fleagle, Bingo, Drooper and Snork'. I know you can pogo to it but gobbing and sticking the Vs up while 'making up a mess of fun, lots of fun for everyone' doesn't exactly make it an anti-establishment anthem.

Anyway, back to Saturday morning TV and the emergence of homegrown programmes like Tiswas (silly and funny), Swap Shop (slightly silly and slightly funny) and the rise of Noel Edmonds and, in due course, his wobbly pink friend (about as funny as ceefax or my 'wobbly pink friend' comment). And what a hypocrite Edmonds was for consistently slagging off Tiswas by dismissing it as a 'worthless gunk-fest' and then later making a fortune by copying the same format for his own show.

The phone-ins were generally pretty anodyne stuff … other than Matt Bianco's appearance on Saturday Superstore, with Mike 'let's not Relax' Read, when a caller named Simon Roberts became an instant hero to thousands of secondary school kids by telling the band that they were a bunch of wankers (another one to google). The two male band members looked mortified, the studio audience (average age seven) were completely non-plussed and the female singer, Basia, just grinned. Judging by her bandmates, she probably agreed with Simon. I assume he's now the music critic for the Sunday Times.

I stopped watching Saturday morning TV once I left school because I stopped getting up earlier than Saturday afternoon but the theme tunes never left me. I reckon most of you reading this would be able to sing any children's TV theme tune from the 70s/80s after hearing the first few notes (I'll name that tune in three, Tom ... or Lionel if you're slightly younger than me ... or Jools if you're not much older than my kids).

There were classics like Rainbow ('paint the whole world with a ...'), Trumpton ('Pugh, Pugh, Barney McGrew ...') and the Gerry Anderson shows (lots of key changes, the odd voiceover and a chorus belting out the name of the show – Stingray, Captain Scarlet, Thunderbirds – at random intervals) as well as some quirky left-field bangers like Chorlton and the Wheelies, Flashing Blade and the Double Deckers.

Listen to them now and be immediately transported back to a time before jobs or marriage or kids, when the toughest questions in our lives were what attracted Maggie Philbin to Keith Chegwin (we hadn't seen him naked at that stage so could rule nothing out), who was under the mask of the Phantom Flan Flinger (it was a taxi driver named Benny Mills apparently – if only we had google back then) and how a mild-mannered janitor ended up becoming the number one super-guy. The only janitors I knew ... well, that's another story I guess.

A friend of mine told me after this story was posted that they'd had their envelope picked out on Multi-Coloured Swap Shop (by Tony Blackburn apparently) and won a selection of Dad's Army items (including a helmet from the show) and an Action Man with swivel eyes. It would've been fine if she was a boy but she wasn't (and still isn't as far as I can tell). The BBC used to be one of the worst offenders when it came to political correctness in the old days but, wow, are they making up for it now.

8 SKATEBOARDING

The absolute very first time I tried to skateboard was in the early 80s, several years after the craze had fizzled out. I knew I'd be crap at it. I've got an appalling sense of balance and naturally struggle to walk in a straight line (as I've tried to explain to several police officers over the years) let alone do it standing on a narrow plank of wood.

I gave it a go outside my house while I was still at school. This was a time when all kids used to play on the street without fear of being run over or molested (well, OK, run over at least). Playing outside was nothing to do with fresh air or exercise but because a) there was nothing to do indoors after 'Why Don't You?' finished and b) You could hear Mr Softee coming more clearly if you were outside (that's the ice cream van not the next door neighbour).

We lived on a road which commuters tended to use as a cut-through and my father, who had to back his car out onto it every morning on his way to work, constantly complained that it was 'like Piccadilly Circus out there'. I'm not sure if Dad had been to Piccadilly Circus (he wasn't a big theatre fan) let alone drive round it but it didn't seem a fair comparison with a sleepy market town with equally sleepy car drivers who didn't need speed cameras, sleeping policemen or radar guns to persuade them to pootle along at least 15 mph below the speed limit.

It wasn't as though there was much of a school run either. Normally, the only kids who travelled to school in a car were ones who'd passed their test and were driving themselves. All the local kids were made to walk or cycle. It's just what you did in the 70s & 80s unless you lived at least ten miles away, didn't own a bicycle or had lost the use of your legs (both of them – one was no excuse).

I lived a mile away from my primary school and had walked there from the age of seven. My mum took me outside one morning, strapped my satchel onto my back, showed me the lamp post where it was safe to cross the road and pointed in the vague direction of the creepy passageway I was supposed to negotiate every morning and night ("you might want to run at night"). If I made it through unscathed (and I'd seen plenty of Scooby Doo episodes to suggest this was unlikely), it was simply a case of 'following my nose' after that. She rounded off the instructions with a cryptic comment about Bob being my uncle even though I thought I already had a perfectly reasonable one called Frank, which hinted at murkier family mysteries than I had imagined up to then.

Over the next four years, I had to run the gauntlet of that creepy passageway twice a day, five days a week through pouring rain ("put your hood up"), blazing sunshine ("take your hood down") and snowstorms ("don't worry about your hood but wear something bright in case we have to dig you out"). If my parents knew what paedophiles were, they certainly thought they didn't exist outside Leicester or Nottingham and, when it came to child abductions, these must have been entirely the fault of kids who foolishly failed to follow their noses once they'd emerged from creepy passageways, regardless of the name of their uncle.

My secondary school was a further mile away so, at the age of 11, I was given the option to walk or take my brother's old bike, the one with the dodgy front brakes. I'd have preferred a Raleigh Chopper but buying new stuff in the 70s & 80s was such a lengthy ordeal – local shops held no stock and had order times of several months – that most people didn't bother. Certainly my parents didn't. Electric guitar? No. Leather jacket? No. Some fuzzy felt and another airfix model kit? Only if it was my birthday and I'd asked for them six months earlier to allow the toy shop time to order them in. The guy who'd go on to found Amazon is the same age as me so I can only assume the situation in the States in those days was much the same as in the UK.

So, I opted for my brother's bike and Mum watched me strap my satchel onto my back, pointed in the vague direction of the main road and waved me goodbye. At that stage, I hadn't learned to ride a bike so the first few journeys were a little hairy. This lack of experience was made worse by the steep hill down to the main road where I had to turn left and merge into the traffic converging on the town from the dual carriageway. I was doing 80-100 mph by the time I reached the bottom, despite frantically squeezing the front brakes which were proving stubbornly ineffective.

Although I only had to manoeuvre past the odd vehicle as I hurtled down the hill, it was a different story when I swerved into the constant flow of cars at the bottom, praying (and I was a budding atheist so you'll get a sense of how bad the situation was) that I'd be lucky enough to slot into one of the wafer-thin gaps in the traffic.

With a bit of practice and once I realised that the front brakes made little to no difference, I used to take the bend without holding onto the handlebars. I'm not kidding. Why on earth I worried about my own kids, many years later, getting hurt on their way up the school steps once I'd dropped them off ten feet away is beyond me. Different times.

Anyway, I've gone on such a lengthy tangent that I forgot I was supposed to be writing about skateboarding. To be honest, there's not much more to say. I borrowed someone's board (no one my age was using them anymore by the time I plucked up the courage to give it a go) and tried to stand up on it four or five times, failing miserably on each occasion. The last I saw of it was as it hurtled, rider-less, down the hill and, missing a wafer-thin gap in the traffic by a whisker, disappeared under the wheels of a Vauxhall Viva heading into town.

I got a comment on the website from a friend saying that her mum had directed her to get to the bus stop down the same dodgy alleyway with the blind dog leg that the mum had been flashed in 20 years beforehand. Nice to know quality parenting was nationwide in the 70s & 80s. For transparency, this was the same friend who'd told me about winning the Dad's Army helmet. She could've written this book herself and made it far more entertaining.

Dance-off!! Me and Rizzo vs Sandy and Danny. We wuz robbed

9 GREASE

The absolute very first time I saw Grease The Movie was when it came out late in 1978. I'm sure it was a film not a movie in those days but, by the late 70s, American vernacular had even made it to my middle England home town (although my mum would've withdrawn my teatime plate piled high with biscuits & sweets if I'd dared to call them cookies & candy – there are limits when you're practising responsible parenting, you know).

Going to the cinema was quite an endurance exercise in those days. The queue for tickets (no, you couldn't bloody buy them on-line in advance) often snaked out of the doors and down the steep and narrow piss-drenched alleyway to the High St below. Some people find the smell of popcorn and hot dogs evocative of the classic cinema experience. I wish.

Abba The Movie (which apparently was an actual 'movie' even in 1978 – that's the Swedes for you) had come out just a few short months before but it coincided with my move from primary to secondary school so might as well have been a lifetime ago. I had been too young to see Saturday Night Fever earlier in the year because it was X-rated (the equivalent of today's '18' which is more accurate but less poetic). The producers had tried to persuade the BBFC (aka the cinema gestapo) to make it an AA (with its age threshold of fourteen) however at 12 years old I looked no more like a 14 year old than I do now – and I'm (well) over fifty – so doubt I'd have been able to blag my way in anyway. My brother had got in to see Jaws (X-rated) when he was 15 but he had a beard and looked 21 so it's not a fair comparison.

Clearly, the same producers had improved their negotiation technique since SNF and somehow managed to secure an 'A' rating for Grease, meaning you were allowed to see it if you were over eight years old. I understand that kids this age nowadays are practically adults but, in the 1970s, this was definitely pre-pubescent. I have no idea what the old farts at the BBFC were on to make them decide it was suitable for eight year olds but they honestly must have been off their tits at the time. Kenickie's condom breaks (which, having not used one up to that point – even to impress my mates by blowing it up on my head – made me assume they were made of plastic), Zuko decides sloppy seconds ain't his style and Rizzo, the leader of the Pink Ladies, skips her period – all interspersed with various references to pussy wagons, gangbangs and flogging your log.

I suspect they'd still have stuck with an 'A' rating even if Coach Calhoun and Principal McGee were shown in flagrante delicto (and possibly even recto) during the National Bandstand Finals. I have watched the film 40/45 times (type that into YouTube followed by Harry Enfield) and can recite 75% of the dialogue off by heart and so can only conclude that it would've helped the BBFC reach a more appropriate judgment if they too had adopted a similar protocol.

When I first watched the film at the cinema, I missed every single sexual innuendo (just like the BBFC but, in my defence, I was 12 at the time) although I'm pretty sure I would've leered every so often at whoever I went with to make them believe I had picked them all up. Unfortunately, I think this might have been my mum. I also don't think it occurred to me that the cast members were all a little too old still to be at school. John Travolta was the youngest at 24 and his girlfriend was born just after the war ended and so could've passed for his mother. If John had known that, two short years later, she would be inviting us to get physical whilst wearing her granny's woolly socks, he would've run a mile.

I read two theories about the film recently (and these are genuine): one is that Sandy really did nearly drown at the beach in the opening scene (hence 'I saved her life …') and the whole film represents her comatose dream, ending with her life support machine being turned off as their car takes off towards heaven in the final scene. A bit like revealing the whole of Dallas Season 9 was Pam's dream of Bobby Ewing's death, except less likely and with better songs. I know it's a bit rich for someone who's watched the film 40/45 times to tell anyone to 'get a life' but I still think I have the moral high ground on this one.

The second theory is that there's an Ancient Egyptian-style curse on the film and many of the cast and crew have met premature deaths or suffered tragic episodes in subsequent years. This is a quote, verbatim, from an article in the Daily Mirror in 2020. I will leave you to make up your own mind. '*However, in the years after the film's 1978 release, whispers of a curse began circulating after so many of the cast, crew and production team were struck down by tragedy. The latest sad news to emerge is the death of actor Edd Byrnes, who played Vince Fontaine in the hit movie musical, who has died unexpectedly aged 87*'. Cut off in his prime at 87? Spooky indeed.

I gather modern commentators are starting to describe Grease as 'problematic' (I've not got my finger on the cultural pulse, I just do a lot of googling to fact-check these stories) which is usually code for 'deserves to be cancelled' so make sure you watch it again before it's re-made to 'reflect the values of today's society'. Expect Danni & Sandy as a lesbian couple, the Pink Ladies re-imagined as the Pink People and the introduction of toe-tappers like 'you're the one that I want unless that triggers you'. And, if it's suitably cleansed to give the 'right' messages, rest assured that the BBFC will no doubt give it a PG rating and encourage bus-loads of nursery school kids to come and see it so that, like the recent theatre production of the 'Family Sex Show', our three year olds can learn about 'boundaries, consent, pleasure, queerness, sex and gender'. Well, you're never too young to learn about that are you?

My Grease album signed by the gang (including John & ONJ). Well, either that or by the same bloke who signed my Smiths album. I'm an absolute sucker for this stuff and am single-handedly keeping some of these eBay charlatans in business.

10 GETTING A JOB

The absolute very first time I got a job (a proper job not a paper round) was at the local market every Friday while I was supposed to be at school. It was thanks to my mate, Stumpy, who had suffered a childhood accident that had left him with a slightly shorter middle finger and this was enough to warrant a nickname which even the teachers tended to use.

That didn't stop him (or me) hauling huge rolls of draylon and cotton in and out of the van for a market stall-holder who fancied himself as a bit of a Del Boy, chirping "lovely jubbly" at his customers and telling them they were "creme de menthe" (which they found hilarious) and calling me and Stumpy "a couple of plonkers" and "a load of chateau neuf du pape" (which they also found hilarious but we didn't).

It was cynical exploitation of the complete absence of HR employment and workplace harassment laws in the 70s & 80s (well, HR anything - it was Personnel in those days and you only saw the buggers when they turned up to fire you) although he abused us both equally, despite Stumpy's disability, so we couldn't fault him there.

Stumpy had discovered a loophole in the school timetable on a Friday afternoon whereby, in place of CCF (the cadet force where mental and physical abuse was legitimised as 'educational' and 'character-building' – think Neidermeyer in Animal House and watch the clip with his horse on YouTube), normal kids (or conscientious objectors) could opt to take on community service instead. This was known as 'granny-bashing' without a hint of malice, affection or humour. It was just the accepted name for community service and even the teachers tended to use it.

Stumpy had worked out that, if you asked the dinner ladies for a sandwich at lunchtime rather than a sit-down meal (and, remember, this was before the invention of packaged convenience food in the chiller cabinet) and then if you had a quick cup of tea with your granny whilst telling her you'd been chatting for hours and relying on mild dementia to avoid any push-back, you could make it to the market stall by 2pm in time to start the afternoon shift.

This was a decent plan but not entirely fool-proof. It required a level of single-mindedness rarely seen in teenage boys and, unfortunately, there were usually a couple of distractions to delay us. Firstly, my home town corralled all of its senior citizens into a small ghetto north of the centre, hemmed in by a large bowling green, the Darby & Joan Hall, the main hospital and several funeral parlours. For some reason that is still not entirely clear to me, ice cream vans tended to patrol this area undeterred by a complete absence on the streets of anyone under the age of 60 until me and Stumpy turned up for our brief visits. It's hard enough as it is to walk past an ice cream van without stopping to order a 99 but there's nothing more pleasurable than doing something you shouldn't when you're supposed to be at school.

Secondly, in the days before the internet, there were only two places where porn mags were readily available – newsagents and hedgerows – and, for yet another reason which remains opaque to this day, the hedgerows around the old people's ghetto were a ripe source of material. And there's nothing more pleasurable than … well, you know the rest.

Despite these diversions, getting to work for 2pm was the easy bit. The morning shift was the tough one. At 16, the last job you wanted was one which started at 6 o'clock in the morning (unless it was a doddle like a paper round). I can count on one hand how often I've had to get up this early for work in the 40 intervening years.

Once was in my early twenties when I had a job in an office near Smithfield Market in London where the pubs would open temptingly early to service the meat packers once they'd finished their night shift. Well, the meat packers and any young lads from the surrounding offices who thought it would be jolly japes to join them for a couple of pints before work which is why me and my two mates turned up at the Hope one morning in our suits and ties for a full English breakfast and some lager tops. I learned three things from this experience: 1. At seven in the morning, three pints of lager tops get you as pissed as a bucket-load in the evening. 2. Hairy-arsed meat-packers do not consider young suited office lads good company no matter how many pints of lager tops you consume and 3. Giggling, making farting noises and coughing "blow job" during the 9am office briefing is not likely to improve your chances of career progression.

Anyway, back in the early 80s, with the cash from the market on a Friday and an equally-lucrative washing up gig at the George Hotel on a Saturday, I was well-placed to splash out at the shops on Sunday. At least I could've done if any of them had actually been open.

In the 80s, the only places allowed to open on a Sunday, even briefly, in my home town were All Saints Church, the paper shop and the pub. Not even Woolies for my fix of over-priced 12 inch Smiths singles and a bag of pick 'n' mix. I had heard of far-flung exotic places – Scunthorpe, Lincoln – where shops were occasionally allowed to open for the whole of the weekend. But, back home, I had to wait until the change to trading laws in 1994 to visit Woolies on a Sunday by which time, in line with most of the UK, I didn't particularly want to anymore.

It's probably why everyone our age coped so well with lockdown. It was basically nostalgia: pubs and shops shut most of the time, kids bunking off school, no foreign holidays and hardly any live sport on telly. Lockdown? That's what was called 'life' when we were younger.

11 SEX

~~The absolute very first tim~~ … nope, not a chance. I've still got a shred of dignity you know.

INSTEAD …

… 11 THE PUB

The absolute very first time I went on a proper pub visit (ie one where I was unaccompanied and which wasn't the local rugby club full of thugs who didn't give a shit how old you were as long as you could down a pint in three seconds) was when I was 14.

The Reindeer seemed to interpret the legal age for drinking differently than most other pubs in my home town. I'm not sure I ever saw anyone in there who was actually over 18. And it wasn't as if we were a profitable target market. We would head downstairs to the space invader machine and make a single pint last the entire evening mainly because, at that age, we liked missile command far more than we did beer.

On the odd occasion, we would sneak down there at lunchtime during school and head back to class afterwards. It wasn't entirely clear whether we were breaching school regulations – we almost certainly were – but, just in case, we would duck out of sight whenever a teacher wandered by the pub although, as this was still during school hours, any teachers who spotted us were just as likely to do the same thing for the same reason. We also made sure we had a ready supply of polo mints on us in the mistaken belief that any alcoholic fumes and cigarette smoke would be instantly neutralised by a hint of minty fresh breath. It also helped our cause if we could offer a pack to any teacher in the same predicament (you know who you are, Mr Earle).

We stopped going to the Reindeer when it changed hands – the landlord presumably aiming to impose his unusual operating model on some other hitherto successful venture – and his successor decided to bring in progressive ideas about sticking to the Over 18s rule and serving food to affluent diners. Commercial suicide or what? He didn't even keep the space invader machine.

My home town used to have 53 pubs when I lived there but it's now down to about three. It's been hard to keep track of the closures. Whenever I've gone back in recent years, I've popped to the pub and invariably found myself marching into someone's living room and being greeted by some precocious ten year old called Primrose or Barney whose mummy and daddy had moved up from London the month before.

One such family now live in what used to be the St Marys pub. It was originally called The Vence in honour of our twin town in France but it was swiftly renamed St Marys once the owners realised that their regulars, all of whom would no doubt vote Brexit 30 years later, would prefer a more traditional name for their boozer.

I had first turned up here on their opening night. I don't think they'd exactly got the publicity machine on overdrive because me and my two mates were their only customers for most of the evening. I took a bit of a shine to Wendy, the landlady. She was classic 80s – big hair and even bigger shoulder pads. I told her she looked like Eve Marie Saint in On The Waterfront, not because I'd seen the film – I hadn't even heard of it – but because, if Lloyd Cole said it, it was bound to be intellectual enough to impress her whatever it actually meant. In hindsight, I think she was more likely to read Jackie Collins than Simone de Beauvoir and I don't think either Lloyd Cole or his Commotions were in her vinyl collection because I've just realised it was still two years before the song came out.

It was clear on that first night with Wendy that there was a spark between us despite the 20-25 year age gap. The Lloyd Cole quote (yes, I know this didn't actually happen but go with me) was a masterstroke and her blank, slightly confused reaction didn't fool me one bit. I could tell she was a lady who liked the athlete in her man and so dropped into the conversation that I played county cricket. I'd piqued her interest. She asked whether it was the U.18s team I played for. My mates were nudging me under the table and whispering something about her being the landlady – bit pointless, duh, she hadn't kept it a secret from me and, if it didn't bother her, it hardly bothered me.

Sadly, it obviously did bother her after all because, as soon as I told her it was actually the U.16s, she kicked me out and told me to come back in three years time. It was a strange act of denial but an important life lesson for a 15 yr old boy on the vagaries of courtship. She let me back in the following week but never showed the remotest bit of interest in me again. Women, eh, am I right?

Nights out in my teenage years, tended to be one long pub crawl, interrupted only by a 99 from the ice cream van on the way down to St Marys and a bag of chips near the end of the night on the way back when the only thing left to round off a successful evening was getting beaten up by skinheads outside the chippy as we headed home. Nowadays, the chippy's gone as well as the 50 pubs but the smell of Doc Martens leather on my nostrils always takes me back to Wendy and a happier time.

One thing I do miss is all the advertising paraphernalia in our pubs. In the old days, we didn't spend our nights out taking selfies or showing each other YouTube videos so the beermats and calendars were actually designed to entertain us. Pubs had this weird notion that making an evening enjoyable encouraged us to stay longer and drink more. You don't see beermats that often these days and any you're lucky enough to stumble upon usually carry messages warning us not to drink too much. Huh? Is it just me or have I failed to spot the joke here?

Here she is as lovely as I remember but perhaps I may have been exaggerating about the shoulder pads. Nice smile … but I took the photo so she's not smiling at me. I'm not sure why all the bottles were there – Ruddles County was the only thing anyone drank in my home town with Theakston's Old Peculier a decent alternative if you wanted something a little more refined (or you were trying to impress your date).

12 GRANGE HILL

The absolute very first time I watched Grange Hill was the first series in the late 70s. It's really hard to explain to my kids how anything which now looks like everything else in popular culture (Young Ones, Star Wars, Live Aid, Sex Pistols etc) was once genuinely different to anything else which came before it. Grange Hill fell into that category too. There just wasn't anything on the telly like it.

The only school most of us had seen on TV before then was St Trinians with its cross-dressing headmistress, organised crime syndicates and institutionalised bullying, all set within acres of rolling Oxfordshire countryside. It was great fun and no doubt Tucker Jenkins and Alan Humphries would've loved to attend it but it didn't look much like my middle England grammar school, let alone an inner-city comprehensive.

Grange Hill did. The series caused controversy when it was first broadcast and was routinely accused of promoting unruly behaviour in the classrooms of Britain. To be fair to the writer, Phil Redmond, the storylines simply mirrored government policy at the time in which the Dept of Education's (DoE's) mission to improve the mental resilience of young people could be summed up by the mantra they borrowed from the German philosopher, Nietzsche (years before Kelly Clarkson had the same idea); 'what doesn't kill you makes you stronger.'

There were so many death traps which DoE policy makers in the 70s & 80s either turned a blind eye to or, as I strongly suspect, positively encouraged that there's enough material for a later story and so I won't cover it all now. Suffice it to say, all toys were dangerous. None of them passed safety tests. All paint contained lead and killed you. Ring pulls on fizzy drink cans were designed to sever fingers and kill you. Cycle helmets were illegal and so there was a fair chance that falling off your Raleigh Chopper would kill you. Even sweets copied things that killed you. Cigarette sticks from Barratts? They made Refreshers, Flying Saucers and Sherbet Dip Dabs for goodness sake! You know they call them candy sticks now (lol, as my kids would say).

To balance this off, the Department for Terrifying the Shit out of Children (DTSC) created the most horrific public information films (PIFs) aimed at young people, most of which were so traumatic that many of us are still receiving counselling 40/45 years later.

Up until then, the scariest thing I watched on TV (besides Dr Who) was the section on Play School where Brian Cant and Floella Benjamin (kids TV royalty) introduced stories through different-shaped windows, one of which – the arched one – I found particularly creepy. My heart would sink if they chose that one over the round or square options. Am I the only one? Oh, I see. What about the toys then? Big respect to Humpty, Jemima and the Teds but that Hamble had almost certainly escaped from the set of the Exorcist.

These PIFS took things to another level though. They were highly effective but were so absolutely terrifying that nothing they targeted could ever be looked upon in a positive light ever again. To this day, I wonder what it would be like to watch a fireworks display and marvel in innocent bewilderment at the kaleidoscope of colours lighting up the skies ... but I can't because FIREWORKS KILL.

Same with frisbees They never seemed to sail serenely between acrobatic and athletic young children but, instead, lodged themselves in power cables which would summarily electrocute the unfortunate kid who climbed up to retrieve them, whilst his young friend beat herself up for not suggesting a more appropriate place to throw the thing around like one of the many open fields they must have trudged through to get to the electricity sub-station in the first place.

At least they weren't down by the river. Many of us can't look at a pond or stream without conjuring up the creepy figure of the Grim Reaper, voiced by the equally creepy Donald 'Blofeld' Pleasence (and who doesn't think, in Halloween, that he was just as scary as the piano music or the nutter in the mask?), as he drowned any kid who so much as glanced at a pool of water … and a generation of Olympic swimmers were lost to Britain as a result.

They targeted old people too, though they had to dream up some pretty niche accidents to scare the crap out of the grannies including the classic 'mat on the polished floor' routine when you've got your son and his new baby visiting ("that old chestnut" I hear you chuckle unless you actually said "wtf??"). The voiceover dripped disdain: "Polish a floor, put a rug on it?" it mocked, "You might as well set a mantrap" and, with that, the cosy hallway mat was replaced with rusting steel jaws, primed to snap shut over the poor unsuspecting young man's ankle.

Even their choice of safety ambassadors was presciently chilling. Jimmy Savile advised us to clunk click every trip or he'd lean over and fix it for us. Rolf Harris taught us to swim ("I'm sure you can guess what it is yet, Rolf, but I'll still float without you putting your hand on it"). Even Darth Vader was employed to teach us the Green Cross Code, reminding us that he wouldn't be there when we crossed the road because he'd be exterminating entire planets in acts of global genocide instead.

Finally, I need to mention the 'Charley Says' series of adverts warning us against dodgy strangers. Although Charley was a crudely-animated cartoon cat with an unusual miaowing technique (courtesy of Kenny Everett apparently), I took his advice to heart and, when my uncle picked me up from cub scouts and offered to show me some puppies, I screamed so loudly that the police were called. My uncle never spoke to me again but, if I'd managed to save just one other child by my actions, then that was a price worth paying.

Back to Grange Hill though (sorry, I tend to get sidetracked). In the first few series, Tucker and his mates encouraged us to throw benches into swimming pools, attempt to enter a foreign country illegally (France – why would you even bother?) and steal antique flintlock guns (was this the Middle Ages?) as well as introducing us to under-age drinking, glue sniffing, graffiti, truancy, numerous fights and some terrific bullying by Gripper Stebson.

I'm sure you can plot a direct line of correlation from the popularity of Grange Hill to the vandalism in the Blue Peter garden. And with their campaigning stand against snitching, you can also thank the programme for the fact that (leaving aside Les Ferdinand's unreliable confession, prised out of him by a sneaky journo) the culprits were never brought to justice. The BBC upped security afterwards but the horse had well and truly bolted by the time they got Jimmy Savile and Rolf Harris to patrol the grounds at Wood Lane. Now, if they'd had that idea in the first place …

13 HITCHHIKING IN EUROPE

The absolute very first time I went hitchhiking in Europe was just after my O-Levels. I'd been hitching in the UK for a year or so by then and hadn't been molested or murdered so I thought it was safe to give it a go on the continent.

In the 80s, hitching, for the benefit of any younger readers, was like Uber except it was free. It's gone out of fashion in the intervening 30-40 years and is probably considered too dangerous nowadays but, back then, my parents didn't bat an eyelid, as long as it saved them from having to give me a lift.

I celebrated the end of my exams by heading down to see some friends in Malaga and then decided to hitchhike to Athens. I wasn't entirely sure where Malaga and Athens were in relation to each other but I knew they were both in Europe so couldn't be too far apart. Up until then, the nearest I'd got to the Continent was skimming stones off Woolacombe Beach on the coast of North Devon and being told by my Dad that they'd gone halfway to Portugal. Geography was never his strong point although he claimed to have studied it at University but, in his day, you were awarded a 2.1 degree in your final exam if you managed to fill in the names of the major cities on a map and colour in the countries without going over the lines.

In Spain, I tended to get lifts from lorry drivers including one who took me on the first leg of my journey, between Malaga and Granada, and tried to have sex with me. Luckily, one of my O-Levels was Spanish and, unlike French, I could speak it pretty well so a constant mantra of "las chicas solamente" (look it up on google translate) and a refusal to touch anything which wasn't welded to the truck (and the thing in front of me didn't even look like it was welded to him) meant I reached Granada intact and unscathed.

With the Schengen agreement still a twinkle in the eyes of Monsieur Mitterrand and his EU chums, crossing a border in Europe was a lengthy and tiresome process which was only made tolerable by the prospect of a stamp in your passport at the end of it (like a sweetie from the nurse after your BCG jab). There was no computer database so the officials just kept you waiting for the hell of it, glancing at your photo (I had spikey, freshly-dyed blond hair, an earring and an attitude so looked nothing like the awkward schoolboy in the photo) and having a good nose through your passport stamps to see where else you'd visited. It was their way of making you think that your chances of being allowed in were 50:50 and would only improve once they'd taken you into the back office and slapped a latex glove on their hand. It relieved the boredom I guess.

Once I'd got into France, it was like being transported into an episode of Starsky & Hutch. All corners were taken at 100 mph, ideally with the hubcaps slamming against the kerb while over-taking some other maniac driver, and any kind of alleyway (ideally a rubbish-strewn one) represented a potential shortcut. All that was missing was someone sliding across the bonnet or landing on the roof (oh, and Huggy Bear obviously). On one journey, I was so terrified that I begged to be dropped off. Luckily, one of my O-Levels was French but, unluckily, I had oublié tout because I'd taken it over a year earlier (I've done a refresher course since as you can tell) and so struggled to deliver this message with the fluency required for it to be understood.

Once over the Italian border and past Pisa, I got a lift in a soft-top driven by two beautiful Italian girls who drove me into Florence with the roof down and the sun blazing overhead, laughing and singing together all the way in. They were in the mood to party and asked me to join them, offering me an evening to remember and a place to stay the night ... which, for some unfathomable reason, I politely but promptly declined and bid them a cheery farewell. I think I've mentioned elsewhere that a small proportion of my stories are exaggerated, made-up or mis-remembered. I truly wish that this was one which fell into that category.

Instead, I headed to a summer school where a friend of mine was studying and where I slept on the floor of a boys' dormitory, ready to roll under one of the beds if the housekeeper ever came in to check. Even my mate would concede that, given the alternatives, this was a decision of mine which ranked right up there with throwing away my Six Million Dollar Man doll in its original box, considering that's about what it's worth nowadays.

Afterwards, I hitched south and took the ferry across to Corfu where a guy gave me a lift and offered to take me out on the town. The next thing I remember was waking up in an empty house halfway down the coast. To this day, I have no idea whose house it was, how I got there and whether I'd happened to pick the one moment when my captor had popped out for some rope and a spade to make my escape. As it was, I wandered out of the house, stuck out my thumb and headed back to the harbour to catch any lift I could find to Mainland Greece. I'd have joined Captain Pugwash and his cardboard cut-out crew of dubiously-named seamen if it meant getting off the island more quickly.

Once I'd had my fill of Athens and rather than hitch all the way back home again, I decided to experience the classic backpacker adventure on board 'The Magic Bus to London'. Nowadays, with social media scrutiny and trading standards, it would simply have been called 'The Bus to London' and I'd have been able to read 50 reviews advising against taking the trip in the strongest possible terms. In those days, if some bloke in your hostel happened to suggest it was 'alright', you were booking a ticket the next morning.

I arrived in London Victoria and thumbed a lift up north to within a mile of my home town, which turned out to be close enough to encourage my mum to pick up the son she hadn't seen for over a month. I know I now had blonde hair and had lost a stone in weight but that didn't really explain why she drove past me twice before deciding to pick me up. I've had Spanish lorry drivers who were quicker to give me a lift than that.

My first passport photo at 14, taken during lunchbreak in a photo booth inside Woolies. It looks like I dropped a cola-flavoured spangle on it before I sent it off but perhaps they thought it was a birthmark so used it anyway. Note the loosened tie and undone top button. There are lots of ways to fight back against the establishment and smash the system. This was mine.

14 LEG WARMERS

The absolute very first time I saw a pair of leg warmers were wrapped around the shapely calves of Olivia Newton John in her video to Physical in 1981. ONJ still had some caché from playing Sandy in Grease having completely reinvented herself after an early career spanning a distinctly uncool cover of Take Me Home Country Roads (which personally – shhhh – I loved) and an equally uncool 4th place finish in the Eurovision Song Contest behind some Swedish no-hopers (and whatever happened to them then, eh?). Not only that but, as I've told you before, she was old enough to be John Travolta's mum by that time so she'd done well to get back into the Hit Parade again.

'Physical' was not exactly a track you'd have found on Side 2 of Never Mind the Bollocks but the song and video were definitely more Sandy than Sandra Dee ('there's nothing left to talk about unless it's horizontally' – what the actual fuck, Olivia!!). This video had all the elements to catapult her back to the top of the teenage boys chart above Pamela Stephenson … until we realised she was wearing thick woolly socks.

Fame hadn't made it to my local cinema in 1980 – neither had the Blues Brothers although I managed to get to see Private Benjamin so not all was lost – but I gather it was leg warming heaven. The TV spin-off series was still a year away so the Physical video was my first opportunity to see a sexy woman wearing thick long socks since I'd walked in on my grandmother by mistake while she was getting dressed.

Leg warmers – along with leotards – became associated with dancing and exercise, neither of which struck me as activities which required such elaborate dresswear. Lightly shimmering to Soft Cell on a Saturday night, as I was known to do (pretty stylishly if I say so myself), was hardly going to work up a sweat and, if you wanted to get fit, that's what PE lessons were for and leg warmers weren't on any approved school gym kit list that I ever saw.

In fact, what you wore in PE lessons relied exclusively on what your mother remembered to pack for you to take to school on the days in question. As many of us experienced – and some still bear the mental scars to this day – if you forgot your kit, you had to take the lesson in your pants and socks (and, if you were lucky enough to be wearing one, a vest). On the odd occasion I've been to the gym more recently, it looks like this is what everyone wears to exercise nowadays but, back in our day, it was absolutely mortifying.

There's an obsession with keeping fit and taking exercise today but, when we were young, I didn't know any parents who consciously kept in shape, other than dads who played competitive sport (and the on-field punch-ups and off-field piss-ups suggested that fitness was not the primary motivation for their participation). If you saw someone jogging down the road, you'd assume they were late for work. If they were wearing the sort of thing which ONJ was sporting in her video, you'd assume they'd escaped from a nearby institutional facility.

We didn't need role models to encourage young people to keep active (which is handy because we didn't have any decent ones). We just did it anyway. Our sporting heroes – Keegan and 'Enry Cooper – sat around in the showers discussing the great smell of Brut whilst our favourite bionic-related TV shows prompted nothing more vigorous than slow-motion sprinting around the playground in the style of Steve Austin and Jaime Sommers. Visually very striking but not much cop when it came to getting fit. I probably drew more exercise inspiration from the Shake & Vac advert.

Anyway, it wasn't the fitness aspect of leg warmers that was the problem, it was when I started to notice friends of mine from the girls school wearing them at parties (and possibly in school too for all I knew). They were not my favourite item of clothing and I obviously still had that shocking memory of granny to haunt me but a) what's it got to do with me and b) I was a new romantic at the time so I'm a fine one to talk.

Leg warmers weren't the worse fashion atrocity of the 80s though – take a bow, jump suits, and thank your lucky stars that Sheena Easton secured that recording contract on The Big Time. Some of the other clothing of the time – stone-washed jeans, fingerless gloves, buttoned-up blouses and pixie boots – actually looked pretty good. This all fell apart when Dexys came along and told us, a little unnecessarily, to come on Eileen. That led to an influx of dungarees and neckerchiefs which might have fitted in around the campfire in gypsy communities but looked distinctly out of place on spotty-faced teenagers outside Our Price or Woolies on the high streets of Halifax.

I was always adamant (no, not him) that 70s fashion didn't have a prayer of a revival but look how flairs stormed back into our lives not so long ago (or was that just me?). It gives me hope that frilly shirts, baggy trousers and winklepickers could join puffa skirts, shoulder pads and pixie boots in enjoying another day in the sun. And, if Eileen's still game, we could make it a party to remember.

Here are my winklepickers, still primed to shuffle across the dancefloor to Visage. The plainer ones on the right were my school shoes and the suede ones on the left were for going-out. Yes, I know they look very similar – I wasn't particularly imaginative. I probably had a similar pair for PE too.

me, 3 inventors and a bloke who looks like hitler

15 BROOKE BOND TEA CARDS

The absolute very first time I began collecting stuff was, being a boy, probably ten minutes after I learned to talk. It's in our DNA. What may not be in our DNA is the obsessive lengths I've taken it to over the years. When you've got an attic full of games like Totopoly, Haunted House, Battling Tops and Treasure of the Pharaohs, none of which have survived from my childhood and all of which have been purchased off eBay in the last couple of years and never played, you know there's something wrong.

I think it was Brooke Bond Tea Cards which started the whole thing off. My mum would hand me the packet of PG Tips she'd bought as though it was a Christmas present (I think one year it actually was). We weren't a big family of tea-drinkers so she would buy the smallest pack size, meaning just a solitary card had been slid down the inside of the carton. Not yet a fully-fledged atheist at six years old (I was a late developer), I would allow myself a little prayer for the card to be one of those missing from my album. It usually wasn't. There were always a few which had lower print runs than the rest because the Marketing people at Brooke Bond were sneaky bastards. Regardless of that (or perhaps because of it), it was an experience of Willy Wonka Golden Ticket proportions.

Incidentally, the packs were not that difficult to open in-store for a more frequent and cheaper way of feeding the collecting addiction and, although I never tried this myself, I suspect I put enough pressure on my poor mother to give it a go. Before long though, Brooke Bond started to wrap the packs in cellophane and that was that. I told you those bastards were sneaky.

News of the meteoric rise in PG Tips sales clearly reached the petrol stations because I remember taking a similar approach with Dad when it came to Shell's wildlife 3-D cards. It didn't matter that there were several other petrol stations closer to us than Shell, nor that all of these were considerably cheaper, I NEEDED TO FIND THE CHEETAH TO COMPLETE MY SET so Dad had to drive to the Shell one to fill up. End of.

The disappointment of finding a duplicate was slightly eased by the knowledge that you could usually persuade Richard and Rupert, a pair of twins at my primary school whose family were clearly phenomenal tea drinkers, to part with the prize target cards or coins in return for any old rubbish you happened to have on offer: a few chipped marbles, a couple of conkers or, if I really wanted the trade, a partially-eaten curly wurly. I think I even convinced them to accept a pet rock as collateral once. I hadn't even bothered to draw a face on it.

Collecting anything which has a limited and numbered series is a nightmare because, if you have OCD (ie you're a boy), it's impossible to stop until you've ticked off each one in the set (by recording it in the secret notebook which you still carry around today and you hide from your wife even if it makes her think you're either having an affair or covering up a porn addiction instead). Damn, TMI.

I was indiscriminate in my collecting: Weetabix freebies and anything which had 'neat wheat mate' written on it ('ok?'), Mr Men books (on the one hand I was a teenager by then but, on the other, this was a numbered set of stuff just begging to be collected), those ridiculously over-priced weekly magazine series where you got the 2nd issue 'free' with the first because that drew you into buying all 150 issues and ending up effectively paying nearly a hundred quid for a book you could find in Oxfam for 25p. 'Unexplained'? Yep, definitely.

My most expensive hobby, though, was collecting Marvel superhero comics which were published in the 60s in the US. My first copies were gifted to me by my friend, Christopher, from primary school. Strictly speaking, he only 'showed' them to me after tea at his house but I knew what he was really saying and so slipped them into my satchel before his mum drove me home.

Over the years, I built an impressive collection of early Avengers and X-Men comics. They soon became recognised as an investment vehicle to rival stamps & coins and I had a choice of selling either my comics or my Smiths singles to finance my time at college. With values growing nicely but likely to plateau, I plumped for the comics and sold them for two grand to a dodgy dealer in Stoke-on-Trent. Sadly, this rate of growth only accelerated in subsequent years, fuelled by the success of the superhero films, and my original collection would now have been able to buy me a three bedroom flat in Kensington. Instead, back in the 80s, the proceeds barely lasted a year of college and were mostly sprayed up the back wall of the urinals in the Baron of Beef.

On the plus side, I have managed to hang on to my original Smiths singles. Their investment track record, as those who've read my earlier post on Morrissey already know, has been a little on the disappointing side but, whilst they wouldn't quite cover the price of that three bed flat (and some guy from Stoke secured it anyway), they'd certainly look nice on the walls.

I reckon I've largely conquered my OCD but it's possible I've simply renamed it. I call it logical to arrange all my books and CDs in alphabetical order (even the ones in the loft) because, the one time my family persuaded me to dispense with this tried and tested system and 'go random,' it caused my daughter to admit that looking for her Dickens GCSE set text was like trying to find a needle in a haystack (ok, strictly speaking she said my book collection was not exactly the British Library and it only took her two minutes but you get my point?).

My other name for this affliction is nostalgia. The 24 Dr Who 1980s promotional cards from Weetabix? Nostalgia. The 11 figures in the Ray Harryhausen set from Japan (he's the special effects guy for Jason and the Argonauts, Golden Voyage of Sinbad, Clash of the Titans etc)? Nostalgia. The 12 Third Eye Marvel black light posters from 1971 which glow under ultra-violet light and which I've rigged up a whole system in one of the downstairs rooms to show to their best effect when I'm on a zoom call? OK, that might be taking things a little too far.

And wouldn't life be easier (well, far more nostalgic at least) if we could trade these things on eBay for some chipped marbles and a few old conkers? Don't worry, I wouldn't be mad enough to part with my curly wurly this time round though, partially-eaten or not.

By the way, I've just noticed that google dictionary disapproves of my jocular use of the term 'OCD,' describing it as 'ableist' and going on to say that 'as a dictionary, we don't want to use words in a way that makes people feel lesser than' (than what? You're a dictionary so is it too much to ask for you to construct sentences which make sense?).

Let's be honest though, being advised about what is or isn't funny by google is like getting lectured about 'hurty' comments by Jimmy Savile's BBC or having blokes decide whether they should be allowed into the Girls Guides or not. What was that? You are kidding me.

16 YOUNG ONES

The absolute very first time I saw the Young Ones was the absolute very first episode in Nov 1982. Pretty much everyone at my school must've seen it, even the teachers, because everyone was doing impressions of the characters the next day at school, even the teachers. I guess with only three channels (Channel 4 had literally been launched only a week beforehand so we hadn't got used to it being an option) it wasn't difficult to promote a new show to a teenage audience when there was bugger all for them to watch otherwise.

On BBC2, the nearest thing to youth culture on offer was the test card with that young girl who, for some reason known only to her and the BBC producers, had decided to play noughts and crosses on a blackboard with a clown. It was hardly compulsive viewing but, on a wet day in the holidays once you'd read Smash Hits and pulled your Rubik's cube apart in an effort to cheat, there was literally nothing else to do except watch telly. If the test card was the only thing on telly, you watched that.

Clearly in a world before smartphones, we all found our own ways of keeping amused. Mine was crawling behind my mum's vacuum as she pulled it from room to room because it blew hot air (presumably unfiltered and full of dust and mites) out of the back and into my face. I also used to eat frozen yoghurt by lightly defrosting the pot in front of the electric fan heater so my spoon wouldn't bend (this was in the pre-microwave era) and I'd pour fairy liquid into the bath instead of Matey because it created bigger bubbles even if it did give me eczema. We've all got our weird habits though, am I right? I can't speak for you lot but at least mine were relatively harmless. They were sadly all true too.

Anyway, back to Scumbag College. Most of you reading this will remember just how different and refreshing the Young Ones was for anyone under the age of 25 at the time. Sitcom offerings, up to that point, had been Terry & June, George & Mildred and The Good Life plus a few racist and homophobic options if you wanted something old school (Love They Neighbour, Ain't Half Hot Mum, Are you Being Served). They were all sexist – even the non-racist and non-homophobic ones – but this was the 70s so only to be expected. Burn the tapes I say.

Porridge and Fawlty Towers were obviously funny but my parents would watch and laugh at them so they couldn't have been aimed at people my age. If they got a snigger out of me, it was a bonus for them. The Young Ones, on the other hand, felt like the only programme specifically for young people which wasn't actually broadcast in the kids teatime slot before the early evening news. I don't suppose my mum and dad ever watched the Young Ones but, if they did, I can be absolutely certain that the chances of them stifling a snigger were about as likely as them staying in their chairs once the national anthem came on at the end of the evening programming (about 10:30pm in those days).

I know no one watches telly anymore except on catch-up but, in the 70s & 80s, it was the glue which cemented a family together (presumably UHU – great brand name). There was only one television set in a house and one telephone line which your older brother or sister was likely to be using for a large part of the evening. Sitting together in front of the TV – all of you actually watching the same programme at the same time as it was broadcast – was a real bonding experience. It gave you something to talk about as a family. Usually this was arguing over who shot JR or Dirty Den and, thanks to Blankety Blank's formulaic seating plan, taking turns to guess who'd be the 'zany celeb' in the middle of the bottom row (usually Kenny Everett).

We got to practice our Mike Yarwood impressions together too. Frank Spencer and Dick Emery were my forte and, if somehow the family managed not to crack up when I launched into my signature "hmmm Betty, the cat's done a whoopsie on the carpet", I'd definitely have them in stitches with a pitch perfect "ooh, you are awful but I like you".

Whilst my Dad seemed content to stick with Dick Emery impressions from then on (he still does them today at 90, much to the bewilderment of the young care home staff who wouldn't know Dick Emery if he shoved them in the chest), I moved on to quotes from the Young Ones which, unlike Frank & Dick, didn't prove quite so popular with my parents.

There were only twelve episodes in total, all of which were forensically dissected at school the following day. I particularly remember the flash frames in series 2 stirring up a few mass brainwashing conspiracy theories. Other topics of interest were Rik, Vyvyan & co breaking the 4th wall (although, in those days, the concept of a 4th wall was yet to catch on so we called it 'talking to the camera') and their obsession with Cliff 'oh ffs he's got the Xmas No.1 AGAIN' Richard. Am I alone in secretly loving the Comic Relief single of Living Doll? Probably.

One nice move was to incorporate the typical light entertainment device of the 'musical interlude' into the actual set for the cast to interact with (Madness, Motorhead, Dexy's etc) because, apparently, that got them a bigger budget from the BBC box-tickers (god knows what they spent it on – fake snot I assume). I particularly liked Amazulu in the first series but the single they played on the show – Moonlight Romance – never even charted so I was clearly the only one who did.

I watched a few episodes again recently and was delighted to find one with video nasties as the main focus. I've not heard that expression since the 80s and have just checked with my kids and they've not come across it at all. Video nasties were a comprehensive record of all the obscene or violent films which the DPP felt ought to be banned in the UK, thus providing an invaluable shopping list for young people to take to their local video shop and hire them out. You could simply go onto the DPP website and print…ohhh wait, it was 1984 so you couldn't.

I wanted to avoid filling up this story with quotes from the series but I have to mention the exchange in the opening scene of that video nasty episode when an old woman (ie someone over the age of 40), pushing a corpse in a wheelbarrow through a cemetery, asks Neil the Hippy whether he digs graves. "Yeah," he replies, "they're alright." Even my folks might have laughed at that one.

17 NATIONAL LAMPOON'S ANIMAL HOUSE

The absolute very first time I watched Animal House was probably not when it was originally released in the UK in 1979. In the previous year, my cinematic journey had taken me from Abba: The Movie to Grease so I doubt I was quite ready for John Belushi by the following spring. Also, I was still 13 yrs old and, at that age, no doubt thought that the Germans really did bomb Pearl Harbor and a toga party was something I would read about at school in my 'Caecilius est in horto' Latin primer.

The boy who eventually watched Animal House a couple of years later though had, in his own 15 year old mind at least, grown up to be a man. Not only had I moved up to the senior school by then but I had also officially become a 'sex person' … not because I had actually had sex but because, as I've mentioned before (so? I'm proud of it), Adam Ant had graciously conferred this title on me in 1980 as a thank you for listening to his Antmusic.

Having Grease as well as Animal House – in many ways, its complete antithesis – as my favourite films shows the difference between 13/14 and 15/16 year olds. I'd just left primary school when I watched Grease and it laid out a future beyond school, a future of romance, true love and the girl I would spend the rest of my life with. Animal House was when I'd entered senior school and so, by then, my aim when I left was simply to have sex with anything that moved.

The language of the film entered the lexicon of our daily lives and whole conversations at school were made up of quotes from our favourite films and TV shows at the time. A prize (ok, a virtual pat on the back) for guessing where they all come from. Answers at the bottom of the page … but no skipping to the end to cheat.

1. "A hickie from Kenickie is like a Hallmark card." "Really? Would you like to rub my tits too?"

2. "She looks too pure to be pink." "Who? You haven't got a sister, you're the classic example of an only child."

3. "Can you guess what I am now?" "A dead parrot" "You're cruisin for a bruisin, you toilet."

4. "Fat, drunk and stupid is no way to go through life, son". "Tell me about it, stud, but don't mention the war". "Why? We're on a mission from God."

I'm reasonably self-aware (for a bloke) so I assume it's blindingly obvious that I made up all that school banter nonsense simply as an excuse to write down a few old quotes I happened to remember. Even worse, I really enjoyed it too. Yes, sad I know.

'Dead Ants' became a recognised shout on the dance floor at our parties. Well, I say 'recognised' but initially we didn't have a clue what Belushi had actually shouted so tended simply to roar something unintelligible which fitted the metre and most people would understand the implications. It was only later that we discovered the cry was 'dead ants' and this then became the agreed set of words at both school (at the Riverside nightclub) and college (throwing some shapes to DJ Vince's Orgasmagroove) to signal a directive to the dancing throng to fling themselves to the ground and writhe on the floor.

For 40 years, I've struggled with this concept of 'dead ants' writhing around. They're dead after all. Perhaps 'struggled for 40 years' gives a slightly misleading impression because it's taken me only five minutes on google to work out that the shout is actually 'gator' (ie the reptile) which I have to concede doesn't sound too much like the phrase I stubbornly believed for 40 years to be my favourite John Belushi line.

I'm genuinely a bit shocked by this – I feel like the Sheriff in Jaws at his "you're going to need a bigger boat" moment. I now wonder if all my college chums back in the day, whenever I let out that crisp rallying cry of 'dead ants' on the dancefloor (something I would do annoyingly often, regardless of which song was playing), would turn to each other and wearily mutter "he means gator, the twat, but let's humour him and go along with it anyway".

In an homage (it's French – silent 'h') to Animal House, I tried starting a food fight at school. However, seconds after my bread roll sailed through the air towards its intended target, Mary the dinner lady slammed her pot of lumpy mashed potato onto the counter and the fight was over before it even began. You didn't mess with Mary the dinner lady and you never told her that her mashed potato was lumpy.

I had more success with toga parties. My first one didn't come along until I got to college but it sticks in the memory thanks to Fiona's unusual but highly effective method of checking the authenticity of your underwear-free toga outfit at the door before she'd let you in.

I also remember a road trip at school – an absolute classic lads booze cruise to Skegness – and I recently decided to share the debauched details with my children. Sod this 'what goes on tour stays on tour' nonsense – I was desperate to prove that I hadn't always been as boring as they seemed to think. Sadly, I simply managed to reinforce all their prejudices because I genuinely couldn't recall a single moment of the trip. Even my suggestion to them that it must have been crazy because I was clearly too drunk to remember any of it was met with a wall of indifference as it was pointed out that this is exactly what happens to me now after a night watching old Top of the Pops re-runs on TV. I'd show them how I used to do the 'gator' if I didn't think it would wreck my back.

Answers:

1. Grease/Not The Nine O'Clock News (easy).

2. Grease/Young Ones (fairly easy).

3. Animal House/Monty Python/Grease/Sweeney (ridiculously over-contrived).

4. Animal House/Grease/Fawlty Towers/Blues Brothers (absolute nonsense).

Me and my Animal House video – if my house was on fire, that video is what I would've saved. My mum and dad would've saved all those plates. When we sold the family home (my folks weren't around anymore – we wouldn't have done it if they were), we had to pay the clearance guys extra to take the bloody things away.

18 EUROVISION

The absolute very first time I remember watching the Eurovision Song Contest was in 1974 on one of the many occasions the event took place in the UK because, in those days, we usually won it the previous year. Our own entry was performed by Olivia Newton John who was an Aussie but qualified as British because of her Welsh dad and the fact that Cliff Richard needed a year off.

Apparently her song, Long Live Love (be wary of any alliteration using 'l' – it's a crap letter), was chosen by the public via postal vote and she didn't get a say in it. That might explain her lowly 4th place because, thanks to Royal Snail Mail, she probably didn't find out what we wanted her to sing until a couple of days before the show. They should have simply let the BBC choose the song as they have done in recent years with such noticeable success (by which I mean none at all).

Nowadays we pay exorbitant sums of cash into the Eurovision coffers to get a free pass straight into the final so that we can be ritually humiliated in front of millions of Europeans rather than quietly fade off the scene in the semi-finals. In the old days, that money would have been handed over in brown envelopes to the judging panel to ensure we reached the Top 3 at least. If we wanted to be guaranteed top spot, we'd send over Cliff and Katie Boyle for a threesome the night before.

1974 was the year that Abba won with Waterloo (no shame there for ONJ although she did finish behind a couple of dodgy Italian & Dutch tunes too). They sang in English so I assumed at the time they came from the UK (ONJ sang in Australian – I'm not joking – so I assumed she didn't). Also, I wasn't particularly well-travelled at that age and Sweden sounded like it was somewhere in Wales ... although I think I was getting mixed up with Swansea (both cold and faraway so an easy mistake to make).

I remember Katie Boyle presenting the show and repeating everything in French which seemed a little unnecessary since everyone watching (and most of the performers) spoke and understood English perfectly well because, ever since the end of World War 2, they had been forced to do so under international law. Making the rest of Europe sing in English was meant to give us an unfair advantage (which we rightly exploited in the 60s & 70s with our string of first and second places) but, in 1974, we met our match with the Swedes who had grown up watching British TV and so could speak the language better than most of us in the UK.

Until a recent rekindling of my interest in the competition (thanks to Terry Wogan and Graham Norton taking the piss out of it), I only paid attention to Eurovision for a relatively brief period in my younger days before I found better things to do on a Saturday night (so, no surprise that I'm watching it again now). This happened to coincide with us taking the competition seriously and entering some absolute classic tunes, all of which either won or were robbed of 1st place by some dubious decisions proving that Greece/Cyprus 'reciprocal douze points'-type deals were alive and well even in those days.

'Congratulations' in 1968 sounded like a sure-fire Eurovision success, even if it was sung by Cliff, but he somehow contrived to lose on home soil to Spain's entry (sung in Spanish – the natives were already growing restless) called 'la, la, la' (that's 'the, the, the' surely?). He even managed to repeat the trick with Luxembourg a few years later (his 'Power to all our Friends' proving ironically accurate) despite the country having a population of just seven or eight people of which only two could actually sing. One of them pipped him to the top spot in 1973 and, amazingly, the other one beat the New Seekers the previous year even though it was up against the majestic Beg, Steal and Borrow. Presumably that's what Luxembourg did and converted it into a massive bribe to win the competition. Despite their victory, they got us to host the event the following year because they were skint which pretty much proves my theory.

The performance in the interval of the show (while the votes are being counted and final financial, political and sexual favours are traded) is meant to be a showcase of the host nation's talent and a chance to show the opposition (by which I mean our European friends obviously) who's boss. Look what Riverdance did for Ireland in 1994. It knocked the spots off every single song in the actual competition and I'm surprised it didn't win regardless of whether it was entered or not.

And which source of cultural and national pride did the Brits use to showcase our considerable talent to Europe and the world in 1974? The Wombles. I'm not kidding. Introduced by Madame Boyle (in French too – Les Wombles – classy), we got to watch a film of some blokes dressed in rat costumes wandering around Brighton and picking up litter before one of them strolls into the TV studio holding up a sign hilariously asking for people to vote for them. If they weren't going to bend the rules for Michael Flatley and the Riverdance crew, they sure as hell weren't going to do it for a bunch of jobbing children's entertainers in fancy dress, no matter how environmentally-friendly they were. By the way, isn't it nice to see us Brits virtue-signalling about green issues long before it became fashionable in the rest of Europe?

It was a bit like Boris (and Becks) on the bus at the end of the Beijing Olympics kicking footballs into the crowd and giving an excellent impression of someone who was promising the world that his city would make a right Horlicks out of running the event four years later and reduce the whole country to a laughing stock (much to the amusement of the Chinese media apparently). Amazingly though, London 2012 ended up being an absolute triumph (so, up yours, Beijing), thanks to dozens of athletes, thousands of volunteers and, our trump card, Danny Boyle (Katie's lad). We weren't so lucky with Eurovision 1974 though.

Our golden era in the competition – Sandie Shaw, Lulu and Brotherhood of Man (no, Cliff, not you, sunshine) – was rounded off in 1981 by Bucks Fizz ripping off some skirts, warning us not to be taken from behind and asking if we'd be making our minds up without being totally clear what about. Despite taking place in an era of relentless lip-synching, the performance was clearly live (with John Coleman giving that old warhorse, Ronnie Hazlehurst, a night off from leading the orchestra) and therefore not as slick as modern Eurovision productions but, let's be honest, the proportion of the song being sung live nowadays is not much more than the 'thank you, Lisbon/Rotterdam/Tel Aviv' at the end.

Clearly, it's difficult to finish this story without mentioning contrasting recent UK performances: James Nilman Newman who managed to score nul points for us in the 2021 competition, partly because of anti-UK sentiment in Europe but mostly because it was such a crap song, and Sam Ryder who was robbed in 2022 by the Russian entry (though sadly not in a song contest). Both reactions to their defeats were heart-warming and many Brits are rightly proud of these latest plucky losers who once again proved we are a nation of folk who don't take ourselves too seriously and are willing to sacrifice ourselves for the greater good.

That said, it would be nice if, every once in a while, we tried to win the bloody thing again by drawing on the spirit of the 70s and sticking a generous wodge of cash into the pockets of the organisers. Failing that, we could threaten to get Cliff to sing our entry. In French. Or just send him around the night before for some 'mistletoe and wine', if you know what I mean.

19 THE ITALIAN JOB

The absolute very first time I saw the Italian Job was not at the cinema in the 60s but a few years later when it made its way to the small screen which, in our case, was housed in one of those massive display cabinets in the corner of the room that was meant to blend in with the furniture but took up several more square feet than the TV set it was trying to disguise.

I watched it again recently (on a bank holiday afternoon, just like the old days) and was genuinely expecting to cringe at an out-dated slice of British cinema but it was so much better than I remembered. My teenage daughter watched it and cringed on my behalf but then she's not seen the Carry On films so doesn't realise that all things are relative when it comes to political correctness in 1960/70s movie-making. She thought it was 'slapstick' and 'obvious' which seems a bit rich for a generation who finds anything on Tik Tok compulsive viewing.

Ok, it's fair to say that the women were objectified, the Italians were portrayed as lazy racial stereotypes and the patriotism bordered on jingoism but frankly (as hockey commentator Barry Davies once said ... about the Germans rather than the Italians admittedly) who cares? The dialogue was hilarious, the cinematography breathtaking and the minis (hardly inconspicuous and so an odd choice of getaway vehicles) gave us one of the iconic movie car chases, right up there with the Blues Brothers ("we got a full tank of gas, half a pack of cigarettes, it's dark and we're wearing sunglasses" which holds its own with "you're only supposed to blow the bloody doors off").

The casting couldn't have been more straightforward. Michael Caine played Michael Caine. Noel Coward played Noel Coward and Benny Hill played Professor ... oh no, wait, he played himself too. Benny was a comedy legend in our household and the Yakety Sax theme tune would always bring the whole family together in front of the TV. It's easy to say nowadays that he was of his era – as though he was Jimmy Savile – but the joke was almost always on him and a pretty harmless one at that. The British public loved him, so much so that he made it to the Xmas No.1 spot in the singles chart (although, on that measure, they were equally fond of St Winifred's School Choir and Bob the Builder). Ernie (who, as we all know, drove the Fastest Milkcart in the West) held off T-Rex to top the charts in 1971. You really ought to google Xmas No.1s in the 70s & 80s – it's the most brilliantly eclectic list, covering the ridiculous through to the sublime with virtually nothing in between. Don't be surprised if it pops up as a story of its own ... in fact, flick a few pages on and you'll see that it does.

But back to the Italian Job. The fact that the 'cockney geezer' movie doesn't feel too dated is largely thanks to Guy Ritchie who re-booted it, many years later, with every single film he ever directed. By the way, don't you love it when our British blokes marry into US celeb royalty and bring them over here to adopt our customs (clearly with one notable recent exception)? I thought it was great that Madonna (Queen

Madge) would turn up at Guy's boozer with her flat cap on. Coldplay's Chris Martin, on the other hand, had mixed success with Gwyneth Paltrow. On this side of the Atlantic, we only want to know what she pops up her vagina if it belongs to Chris and we certainly don't want to buy one off her website.

The treatment of women in the Italian Job is pretty dodgy though. From a girlfriend who secures hookers to greet Charlie's release from prison to the Professor's obsession with the larger lady, the female characters are not exactly three-dimensional and empowered. We had a mixed bag of female role models on TV in those days based, no doubt, on the Jerry Hall mantra about a maid in the living room, a cook in the kitchen and a whore in the bedroom. There was Hattie Jacques, Fanny Craddock and Raquel Welch. You wouldn't want to get those three mixed up now would you?

Talking of stereotypes, the song at the end of the film was bizarre. Called 'Get a Bloomin' Move On' but known to the rest of us as the Self-Preservation Society song, it's just a long list of cockney rhyming slang. Almond rocks, daisy roots, Hampstead Heath, whistle & flute, Gregory Peck and plates of meat all get a mention without pretending to make any sense. A no-prize (any of you read Marvel comics in the old days?) for getting them all correct.

Michael Caine is not the only one who's had a brush with the Italian carabinieri (that's police for all you non-linguists). I got arrested in Venice while I was at college. I covered it in my debut/final novel The Lost Muse which was briefly an Amazon best-seller ... in my home town because my mum ordered a box-full. It's a fictional story about young love, early death and the race to discover one of the lost masterpieces of classical literature. Sadly, it was a race which not a huge amount of people were particularly interested in so there are a few copies left on Amazon if you're interested? Go on, make an old man happy.

There were a bunch of us staying with our mate, Chris, who'd somehow got the use of an apartment in a posh block filled with politicians and diplomats alongside the Grand Canal. It would be fair to say we'd been a little noisy and a couple of us might have thrown up out of the window onto the balconies below. Despite heavy drinking, this was almost certainly the result of Tyrolean flu which was rife in those days – don't forget this was in the 1980s, well before face masks were made mandatory, so we were sitting ducks for air-borne infections at the time. One morning, we were woken by armed police who rounded us up and frog-marched us to the station because one of the diplomats had become convinced that a bunch of terrorists upstairs were planning an assassination attempt on his life. Note to self: avoid loud music and vomiting in future terror plots – it's clearly a classic give-away.

We managed to avoid incarceration because I channelled my inner Michael Caine and got me trouble and strife (well, girlfriend) to let the ducks & geese get a butchers of her thruppennies and, would you Adam & Eve it, they let all of us dustbins go. We were such jammy merchants. Guess them or google them. Get them right and, I'm ashamed to admit, that's pretty much exactly how it happened.

Michael and his mates were less fortunate in their own cliff-hanger ending. The Brits at one end of the coach and the gold at the other. No mobile dog and bone in those days to call for help but I'm reliably informed that running the engine to drain the fuel tank in the back of the bus should've done the trick. That would've allowed us to enjoy the ending the film deserved: the Mafia turning up to chase our heroes around the mountain on foot – in classic Benny Hill speeded-up style – as the credits rolled and Yakety Sax played in the background.

After posting this on the website I was trolled on Facebook (yes, I know, wtf??!) by someone who took great exception to my alternative ending and told me in no uncertain terms that the original was better. If writers like me manage to slip through the social media hate crime algorithms, thank goodness there are guys like this who'll still hold us to account.

20 THE TUBE

The absolute very first time I watched the Tube was in November 1982. This particular month was a watershed for young people in Britain with Channel 4 (and the Comic Strip Presents) launching on Tues 2nd, The Young Ones on the 9th and The Tube sandwiched between on Bonfire Night. We'd already had the Falklands War, our fastest goal in the World Cup and the launch of the 20p piece (and, gasp, it wasn't round) earlier that year so a flurry of convention-defying firsts in November just seemed par for the course by then.

The Tube was a moment of revelation for all the teenagers in the country who had been weaned on a diet of Top of the Pops since they were old enough to press the on-off control on the TV set (there was nothing more 'remote' than that). It was the moment we realised that most of the bands on TV were miming to their songs, usually badly, and could actually be allowed to play live … though sometimes pretty badly too.

On TOTP, the audience looked as though they were barely interested in the music and had simply been rounded up from a local Sunday School meeting a few days before. The only ones who were dancing themselves silly and appeared to be enjoying themselves were ten years older than the rest of the crowd and were paid to do so. The live audience at the Tube studio actually looked like they were there to watch the bands. Some of them even danced. For free. Sure, there was the odd tank top and bum-fluff moustache but, even allowing for these fashion faux pas, this was clearly an audience which looked far more likely to have previously attended a live gig than any of the rock concert virgins shuffling about and staring at the cameras on the set of TOTP (which was later described by Dame Janet Smith, in her report for the BBC, as a cesspit of sleaze, making it sound far more interesting than it really was).

In hindsight, TOTP was shite. It's incredible that it brought in such high audience numbers which demonstrates just how few entertainment options young people had at the time. Don't get me wrong, I loved it. I thought it was cutting edge stuff in the 70s but, to be fair, I only had Cheggers Plays Pop to compare it against. I never watched the Old Grey Whistle Test because a) I honestly believed it was a show my grandad was supposed to watch because it had the word 'old' in the title and b) it was on way past my bedtime.

If anyone's been watching Guy Garvey's nostalgic round-up of 70s/80s TV musical gold recently ('From the Vaults'), you'll know that there were some fantastic regional programmes which showcased live music and emerging talent in those days. I genuinely never knew about these until I saw his programme earlier this year because I was neither northerly nor southerly enough to be able to watch them. 'Look East' was our regional programming and the rest of the title, 'because there's fuck all else to do here', was both unsaid and understood.

But, TOTP on Thursday nights was essential viewing if you didn't want to be a social outcast in the playground on a Friday morning.

I'd been reasonably happy collecting skills badges at Cubs on a Monday night but, when I graduated to Scouts and found out it was scheduled for Thursday evenings, I had no choice but to hand in my toggle and badges ... well, not the Outdoor Challenge one obviously – it had taken me bloody ages to build that shelter out of twigs, grass and all the spit I could muster so I still wear it today.

By the way, I got my first ever love bite from Caroline who lived just a few doors down from the scout hut. Just to be clear, she was my age and went to the girls school. She just happened to live nearby. She wasn't Akela or old enough to be my mum. That would've been weird.

TOTP was typical of the BBC in the 70s and early 80s. It purported to be aimed at kids but was produced by old farts and made in the prevailing style of every other light entertainment programme at the time because BBC executives had no idea what young people wanted to watch (or, if they did, they decided it wasn't good for them). Pans People and Legs & Co wouldn't have looked out-of-place on the Val Doonican Show so why on earth were they on a yoof music programme? The BBC got them to dance to songs by T-Rex, David Bowie, Sex Pistols and the Clash. I'm not joking, I just watched them all on YouTube so you don't have to. That's something I can never unsee. You're welcome.

As an aside, I re-watched some Porridge episodes during lockdown (there was bugger all else to do) and those TOTP dancers remind me of a classic Ronnie Barker quote in the series when he tells the young Godber about "them dolly birds that dance on Top of the Pops. What are they called? Pan's People. There's one special one - beautiful Babs [pause] dunno her name though". Ba-dum tish.

As opposed to the painfully scripted and choreographed lines on TOTP, you never quite knew what Jools and Paula would get up to on the Tube and it seemed pretty clear that they didn't either. Unlike the Word, their later replacement which was knowingly anarchic and amateurishly inept, the Tube had a sense of natural confidence and genuine spontaneity.

It also played a role in some of the key cultural events of that era. Bob Geldof contacted Midge Ure on the set of the Tube to discuss the response to Michael Buerk's footage of Ethiopia and, as a result, Band Aid was born. Slightly less significantly – but a minor cultural landmark nonetheless – Trevor Horn spotted an early Frankie Goes to Hollywood demo on the show and signed them up to his label. Mere weeks later, as I've reminded you before, the whole nation was learning to relax when they wanted to come and Mike Read was drafting his complaint to the Radio One bosses who would spinelessly acquiesce to his request for a ban thereby propelling Relax to the top of the charts for a solid five week run as No.1.

The Tube came to an end when Jools proved he was Cool for Cats and cemented his place in the nation's hearts by telling viewers in a live trailer for the show to 'be there or be ungroovy fuckers'. Unfortunately, the execs at C4 didn't find it quite as endearing as we did and the show was cancelled soon afterwards.

Many TOTP peer group presenters slagged off the Tube at the time ('smug, rubbish and smutty') so, nowadays, it's interesting to see Jools officially recognised as a national treasure alongside Judi Dench and Stephen Fry whilst the likes of Andy Kershaw, DLT and Jimmy Savile haven't fared quite so well in the court of public opinion. Bunch of what? Yes, you're right ... and very ungroovy ones too.

This was posted on my website by an old schoolfriend of mine: "I went to university in Newcastle and knew someone who worked at Tyne Tees TV so got free tickets to the Tube every week. There was one episode where I was filmed dancing to Teardrop Explodes. I had a big floppy quiff at the time and thought I was incredibly cool. I got loads of people round to my house to watch it when it was broadcast. Unfortunately, I had chosen to wear a knitted Norwegian sweater that night and it was so hot under the lights I was sweating like a gypsy with a mortgage. My hair was plastered to my head (I looked like I had been swimming) and my face was as red as a tomato. I thought I was having a stroke. I met Paula Yates afterwards and she smelt like the porta-loos at a festival – a mixture of chemicals, alcohol, piss and shit". That's such a beautiful story, James. Thanks for sharing.

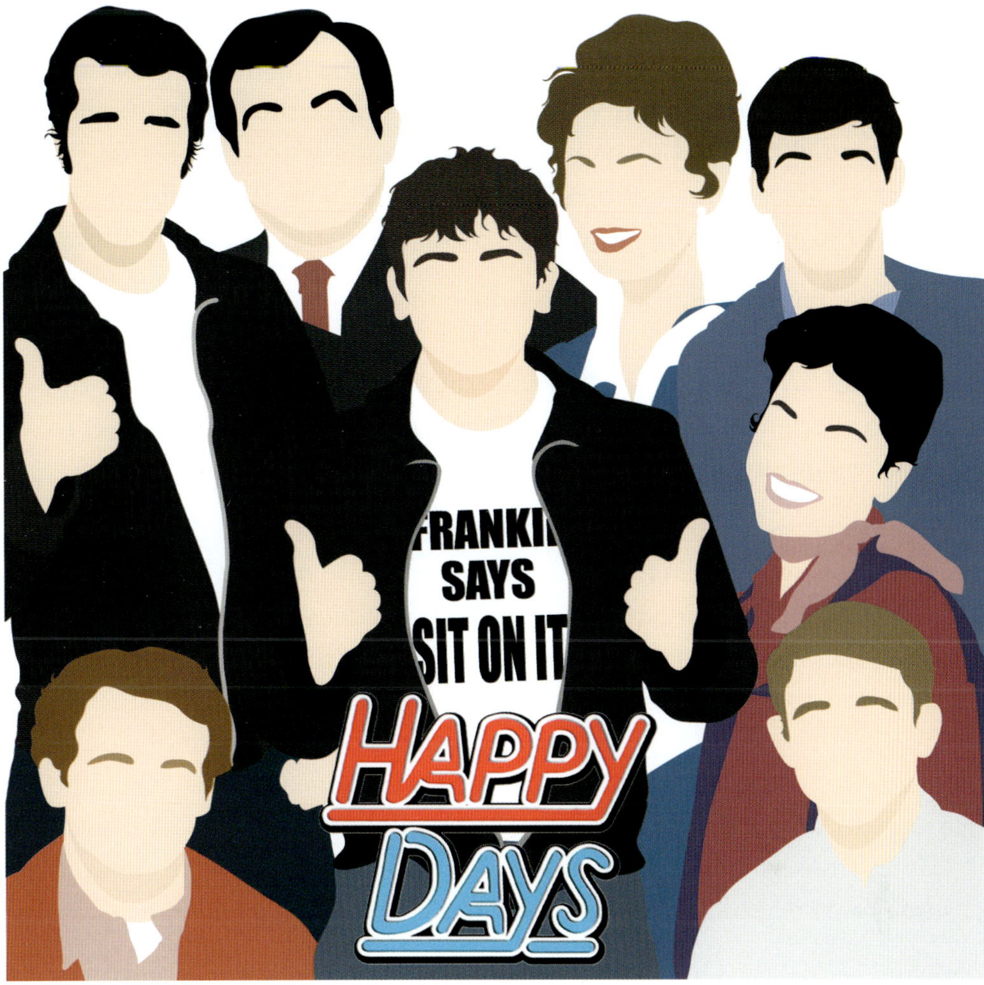

21 HAPPY DAYS

The absolute very first time I watched Happy Days was in the mid 70s when I was still at primary school. I really hope that's true because, pretty soon afterwards, I went out and bought a 'Fonzie' belt and this needs to have happened before I'd reached puberty otherwise I'll be mortified. It had 'Fonz is Cool' written on it so that I could be reminded of this simple fact of life (as if I needed to be) every time I put on my hand-me-down Y-Fronts, pulled up my flared trousers and fastened the plastic strap. I didn't have a girlfriend at the time. Or any friends to be honest. You may not be totally surprised.

Happy Days was on ITV which was forbidden viewing in my household but I told my mum that it was on BBC2 (none of the family watched that channel so I had a chance of getting away with it) and that the "adverts" (not sure if air quotes had been invented by then but I'm sure she got the gist from the tone of my voice) were just part of the show.

Everyone remembers the theme tune and the opening credits, full of 1950s American iconography. You didn't fast forward over the opening credits for any show in those days – they were an integral part of the whole experience. Well, you couldn't anyway because VCRs were yet to be invented but still.

For the youth of Britain in the 70s, Happy Days turned out to be essential viewing to enable us to make any sense out of Grease which was due to hit our cinemas later in the same decade and would share several striking similarities with HD. Luckily not too many though. Did I mention that ONJ was old enough to be John Travolta's mother in Grease? Oh yes, I did … on at least a couple of occasions. I'm obviously obsessed with the age difference. Well, now imagine if Fonzie had gone round to the Cunningham household only to find Mrs C in black leather trousers and high heels, suggesting he should "tell me about it, stud". You'd never look at Grease or Happy Days in the same light again.

Before I leave the Grease connection (sorry, it's my favourite film), it's worth mentioning that Sandy & Danny were nearly played by Marie Osmond and the Fonz himself. I gather Henry Winkler mulled it over before turning it down. Or the producers worked out he couldn't actually sing – one or the other. If the dice had landed differently, we could have had Marie's brothers as the T-Birds. Little Jimmy (who neither had long hair nor hailed from Liverpool but was indeed little) could've passed as Putzie or Doody but I'm not sure I can quite buy squeaky-clean Donny as Kenickie busting his condom and shagging Rizzo at the Drive-In. A little less puppy love and no doubt a lot more doggy-style.

Apparently Fonzie wasn't the original star of Happy Days and it was meant to revolve around Richie Cunningham (or Cun-NING-HAM as the Fonz called him), and his friends Potsie (Potsie/Putzie – another Grease link – oh damn, I've got that image of a leather-clad Mrs C in my head again) and Ralph Malph. I wasn't a big fan of Ralph's (he was a ginge after all) but I've just realised that, when I tell my kids "I've still got it" after delivering a crap Dad joke, that's a direct lift from the Malphmeister himself. All the moments in the show which stay with me, though, involved Arthur Fonzarelli – poised to comb his hair in the mirror until he realises it's perfect as it is, banging on the jukebox to start the music and not letting five minutes go by without a "whoaaa", "heyyy" or "correctamundo". Just as often, he'd tell people to "sit on it" but, because it was a family show, they weren't obliged to swivel as well.

Then there were the finger clicks he used to summon the girls. We never see Happy Days re-runs nowadays and I assume this is because it's fallen foul of the stringent social mores of today and joined 95% of anything which was ever vaguely enjoyable in the dustbin of cancel culture. We need to delete ALL pre-2010 entertainment programmes if that's the case … what was that? Oh, we already have.

The show gave the expression 'jumping the shark' to the world (and, when I say 'world' I obviously mean US TV executives) to signify a moment when a long-running but flagging TV series attempts to use a stunt to re-energise the show but only succeeds in highlighting its irrelevance. Fonzie. On water skis. Jumping over a shark. With his brown leather jacket on (Fonzie not the shark – now that would be truly ridiculous).

More ridiculous still, the show spawned a spin-off series, Mork & Mindy, which was the story of an alien who taught us all to tweak our ear lobes and chirp "nanu nanu" in the playground. In Happy Days, Robin Williams' Mork first appeared in Richie's dream but I've just watched the Mork & Mindy pilot episode where Fonzie makes a guest appearance and teaches him to kiss (in theory, not practice – this was long before boy-on-boy action was made mandatory on TV). I'm not kidding. "Got a guy [pause] got a girl [pause] put their lips together and sort of slide them around" (what, no tongues?). He then invites Laverne round to give their shellshocked visitor from another planet some actual lessons. Both of these weird episodes came out at a similar time so I'm not sure why 'jumping the shark' was adopted as the death knell of a TV show and not 'pimping the alien'.

Besides a karate-kicking Tom Hanks, the other slightly surprising guest appearance came from Suzi Quattro who played the aptly-named Leather Tuscadero (this was clearly a 70s thing – think of the Bond girls; Pussy Galore, Plenty O'Toole, Xenia Onatopp and, amazingly, Holly Goodhead). Rather more far-fetched than her name though was the fact she fell for Ralph Malph. No way!! I bloomin' loved Suzi Quattro (cf Rik's obsession with Felicity Kendal in the Young Ones) and was furious that she'd have the hots for someone who looked like Ed Sheeran (or how I imagined Ed Sheeran would look 35 years later). On the plus side, it probably gave me a glimmer of hope that I might have a shout with her if ever we bumped into each other ... something which I tested when I turned up at a small bar in Adelaide, Australia where she was playing a gig in the mid-80s. She managed to ignore me until halfway through 'Can The Can' before eventually ordering the bouncers to chuck me out. Playing hard to get, the little minx.

I met Henry Winkler too a few years ago. He'd written a series of books about dyslexia and signed them for my son and daughter. He spelled his name correctly (which made me instantly suspicious that this was all just a publicity stunt) but he was a lovely bloke and spent lots of time with my young kids, showing a genuine interest in what they were learning at school and offering them titbits of advice. That said, he declined to give me the thumbs up and say "heyyyyyyy" while I videoed him no matter how many times I asked. He wouldn't even try on the Fonz is Cool belt I'd brought with me. Completely up himself, am I right?

22 PLAYING IN A PUNK BAND

The absolute very first time I played in a punk band was a single audition in the early 80s when punk had begun to disappear elsewhere in the UK but was just filtering through to my middle England home town because our local record stores were run by long-haired hippies who still loved prog rock and would stubbornly refuse to stock anything which had the word 'bollocks' on the cover (it was "uncool man"). The Sex Pistols were right to warn us: never trust a hippy.

At school, we had a couple of decent student bands and I tried to get into both of them. At that time, my instrument was my voice and it was good enough to make me Deputy Head Chorister at All Saints Church. Let's be clear, you don't get to be Deputy Head Chorister at All Saints Church without being able to sing like an angel … unless, that is, you are a personal favourite of the local vicar and agree to additional Sunday School lessons on a 1-2-1 basis.

For some bizarre reason, my potential bandmates failed to recognise how my choral experience could bring a fresh dimension to their screeching punk lyrics. I tried explaining the exciting commercial potential of an Aled Jones/Johnny Rotten mash-up but it fell on deaf ears (or it may have been that they'd never heard of Aled Jones because he didn't sing about child-snatching flying snowmen until a few years later).

Fortunately, there was a third band called Plutonium Babies which my mate, Stumpy, had put together. It had one song, Cinq Minutes, and a drummer whose teachers were so sure he'd fail his English O-Level that they gave him UB40 forms to fill in instead of revision to help him sign on the dole as soon as his results came in. James W had somehow sneaked into the line-up because they wanted a synthesiser and, being a budding electrical engineer, he had made one in his Dad's workshop at home. James would not go on to make a living in electrical engineering because the synth blew up one evening when he was practicing the tricky chords to an early Depeche Mode cover (surely that can't be right?) and took most of his right arm off.

[I should add, in all transparency, that I contacted James before publishing this and he told me that I had got the band members wrong, the electrical accident had actually involved dodgy disco lighting and he didn't even own a synth let alone build one. Most importantly of all, it was HIS band not Stumpy's – the capitals were in his email – and so I decided to leave my version as it was just to piss him off, not least because my wife thought his message was funnier than anything I'd actually written].

Anyway, Stumpy asked me to (ok, eventually agreed to let me) audition and got me to sing their signature song. It started with a dystopian view of impending catastrophe ("you don't seem to realise just how long you've got to live") before an entirely unnecessary synth solo by James 'I was the lead guitarist, honest' W – more Vinnie Jones than Howard Jones – took us into the song. The chorus consisted mainly of repeating the phrase "cinq minutes" at regular intervals but French wasn't my best subject at school and so it took some time to master. I thought a cheeky descant would elevate the song to musical gold but the rest of the band, neanderthals, couldn't recognise a new musical genre if it smashed its mini into a tree in South West London (or choked on a ham sandwich or asphyxiated with an orange in its mouth – bonus points for identifying the rock stars concerned) and they out-voted Stumpy, or so he told me on the phone later, and turned me down.

I knew, to break into the big time, I needed to add a musical instrument to my voice. The only one I'd ever learned at school though was the recorder. Nowadays, school kids have taken Grade 8 in the saxophone, bassoon and double bass before they've even entered primary school but, in the old days, we were offered the recorder or the triangle and I was crap at both of them. When I played 'Morning Has Broken,' I gather my music teacher told the staff room afterwards that it wasn't just broken, it was completely fucked. Harsh.

With hopes of musical success fading, I would sit in front of Opportunity Knocks and cling onto the dream that, one day, Hughie Green would do his slightly weird eye-rolling thing in my direction and announce, most sincerely, that the clap-o-meter had rated me top ahead of Bonnie Langford, Lena Zavaroni and Paul Daniels (whom I liked ... not a lot). I would obviously then have to wait for the postal vote ("in your own handwriting" Hughie would warn us – how on earth was he going to police that one?) before my victory could be confirmed.

At that stage, we didn't know that this Canadian serial womaniser and Nazi sympathiser (we didn't have Wikipedia in those days otherwise that would've been at the top of his bio) had fathered most of the younger TV presenters around at the time (we eventually found out about Paula Yates but there were definitely a couple of the Blue Peter contingent who looked a bit like him too) and, worst of all, had unwittingly provided the show format which would make Simon Cowell millions with Britain's Got Talent. For that, if nothing else, he should never be forgiven.

I've tried to rectify my musical failure in later years. My own kids are guitar maestros so I thought I'd take some lessons myself when I got past 40 so that I could jam with them and make their day. If the jam session was with their mates as well, then they were bound to love it even more. Apparently, they tell their friends that I'm 'sick' and, although this normally means 'brilliant,' they assure me that I can take it more literally when they say it about me.

I got taught by a name-dropping ageing hippy who had allegedly played with Jimi Hendrix/Eric Clapton/Jimmy Page (delete as appropriate). I was still crap at it. He would light a couple of joss sticks and spend most of the lesson playing his own guitar and ignoring me. I paid £30 for the privilege.

I graciously admitted defeat after two excruciating lessons although I vaguely remember him refusing to teach me any longer once I'd told him that Johnny Marr was a far better guitarist than all the old dinosaurs he loved. It was a bit insensitive of me I know – they were personal friends of his after all.

And now my life has come full circle and I'm being denied a second shot at stardom by my own kids who routinely turn down my requests to sing BVs (that's backing vocals for those of you not in the industry) with their own bands. I've got a feeling my choice of choral hymns didn't help my cause in the audition process. When will I ever learn? You can take the man out of the choirboy but not the choirboy out of the man ... apologies, that didn't quite come out as intended.

23 DANGEROUS TOYS

The first time I handled a dangerous toy was no doubt a few days after I was born because, in the old days, every toy in the UK was a potential death trap and deliberately geared to kill us or, failing that, maim us at the very least. If we were merely badly injured, the toy manufacturers and their political masters would consider that an opportunity missed.

Surely, besides their lethal nature (a fairly significant downside I grant you) there have been no finer couple of decades for toys than the 70s & 80s? They had a captive market in young people because there was genuinely bugger all else to do but play with stuff.

I have already explained in an earlier story how it was educational policy to toughen up the character of the nation's youth by deliberately making life hard for us. Parental beatings, teacher canings and school bullying were all actively encouraged by successive governments with subliminal messages which were broadcast in the middle of the news or during the test card (what were they testing by the way – our patience?).

All products advertised specifically to children needed to be exclusively unhealthy or, preferably, downright dangerous. Sweets were produced, under a government-sponsored think tank called 'Barratts,' which looked like cigarettes and were heavily promoted to encourage us to take up the habit once we'd moved up to secondary school. Space dust had an ingredients list like a chemistry set with a full bag of sugar liberally sprinkled on top. All toy soldiers were made with poisonous paint and adverts encouraged kids to lick them when their parents weren't looking.

Jumble sales and church fetes were only granted licences to operate if they contained at least one stall with a wire loop game which administered an electric shock to any unsuspecting kid whose shaky hand meant they brushed the wire with their prong (sounds like a life lesson for lots of young boys). It was later adapted to make a simple buzzing sound on contact but this was a temporary measure until the clergy and parents had left the stall, at which point they'd reconnect the electricity supply to make it a fully-functioning torture device again.

Officials also recruited secondary school kids to set off slinkys down the stairs and see how many of their class-mates they could trip up along the way. These kids were paid on a commission-basis with the biggest payouts reserved for the most serious injuries. My friend Polly commandeered the tallest flights of stairs and made an absolute fortune. She works with horses now. I suspect they do what they're told.

We weren't safe in the shops either. The government appointed Clarks (yep, the evil shoe empire) to create an automated foot measuring device which included a safety switch that could be turned off by the local council allowing the clamp to crush the feet of unsuspecting youngsters in front of their parents. If the Chinese market had been as developed for business back then as it is now, Clarks would've been a great British export success story.

School authorities, in fear of a poor OFSTED inspection or whatever the equivalent was in the 70s/80s (almost certainly nothing), would bow to government pressure and organise British Bulldog games at break-times with the explicit aim of injuring as many kids as possible in the shortest possible time. Our primary school record was 11 kids in 15 minutes, three of them hospitalised. I think that put us mid-table for Lincs and South Kesteven but well behind the progressive schools down south.

Another cunning plan from the administrators was to paint an absurdly large hopscotch grid on the playground which required leaps of such prodigious lengths, well beyond the capabilities of 8-11 year olds, that the school was bound to chalk up a couple more casualties in afternoon break to add to the total.

We were such an obedient generation. Advertisers could make us do anything in those days and we were absolute suckers for it because we were so media illiterate. We didn't understand their cynical marketing tricks and we dutifully did what anyone on telly suggested, especially if they were celebs whom we assumed had only agreed to take on these advertising roles because they genuinely believed in the product and not simply because they were bunged a few quid. When they said we should tell our mummy about the honey but not about the high levels of sugar in our 'healthy' cereal, we did as we were told and sales of Sugar Puffs went through the roof. Our folks would've done the same with Campari if they hadn't been put off by anything which might have wafted here from Luton Airport.

Faced with a drink which was so full of additives that it glowed in the dark and required polar bears to wear sunglasses in the adverts, we ignored the fact it tasted awful and was probably taking years off our lives. After all, it was 'frothy man' and this outweighed any other downsides in our innocent minds. And don't get me started on weebles which wobbled but didn't fall down. You'll know by now that I was never particularly impressed with this as a marketing concept. That said, I bet if I'd have presented one to my son for his birthday when he was younger (and this was as destructive a four year old as you could possibly meet), there's no way that thing would have managed to get back up again

As in every sci-fi big brother movie set in a dystopian future, there was always the usual small group of safe toys which slipped through the policy net. Fuzzy Felt, airfix models, hula hoops, scalextric, sea monkeys, shaker makers, space hoppers, sketchagraph, swing ball. All of them offering a glimmer of hope for brighter times ahead and many of them beginning with the letter 's' (come on, conspiracy theorists, surely a sign?). Like todays iPhones, we would spend hours on these toys but, unlike iPhones, we couldn't use them to watch porn, send nude pics or abuse people we'd never met before. Clearly, and I may only be speaking for myself here, if we could've, we would've.

Nowadays, toys and games are screened so rigorously to protect our children's physical and mental well-being that anything which threatens to entice kids off their backsides has been banned. Skipping ropes, yo yos and conkers are all viewed as too dangerous while egg & spoon and sack races are overly-competitive and so damaging to the self-esteem of any kid who fails to win (referring to a child 'losing' is now officially considered a hate crime).

To balance this reduction in activity and tackle the inevitable obesity issues it causes, we're trying to stop them eating any snacks which taste good. What's more, to address their mental health, we've replaced these snacks adverts with promotional material for Play Station and X-Box games where they can shoot, run over or stab anything which takes their fancy in the most gruesome of ways from the comfort of their own bedroom. Suddenly, cigarette sweets, sugary space dust and lead-painted toy soldiers don't seem quite so dangerous after all.

Some bloke told me on the website that, if I thought Scalextric was safe, I'd clearly never run my tongue across the transformer contacts before. That made me laugh. They'd come with a public health warning nowadays as an arse-covering exercise for just such an eventuality.

24 SPORTING CLASSICS

The absolute very first time I watched a sporting classic was probably the World Cup Final in 1966. I was born by then but hardly old enough to argue about whether or not the ball had crossed the line although apparently my Dad suspected that I had controversially queried the Russian linesman's decision and so dispatched me to the doghouse as a result. This, in our case, was a cold outdoors kennel next to the guinea pig hutch at the bottom of the garden but that's how your parents taught you a lesson in the 60s, even if you were nine months old and had simply got a bout of colic at the same time as Hurst's shot came down off the bar.

By 1970, I still wasn't really old enough to appreciate Gordon Banks' save from Pele's header or work out how Chelsea's Peter Bonetti had dumped us out of the World Cup (he didn't play for Germany – he was our reserve goalie). And afterwards, we never made it to the finals for another 12 years thanks to a Polish 'clown' of a goalkeeper in 1974 (I wish Bonetti had been as funny) and a lack of goals against the European powerhouse that was Finland in 1978. Even then, Spain '82 was a blink-and-you-missed-it affair (much like Kevin Keegan's header in our final game) and my formative years came and went without the excitement of a major tournament run thanks to Keegan's hairdresser and the extravagant ball-deflecting perm he created.

I was sports-mad in my younger days. Summer holidays in North Devon were spent either playing beach cricket (just in case you didn't believe me when I told you before, Dad really would encourage other families to join in so that he had someone to go to the pub with later) or listening to Test Match Special in the wind-swept sand dunes of Woolacombe Beach which is where I first heard that the bowler's holding the batsman's willy and thought this cricket lark sounded like a bit of a laugh.

My favourite sporting moment has to be Botham's Ashes in 1981. The cricketers England produced in the 70s & 80s tended to be as exciting as watching grass grow (although, when Boycs & Tavare were batting on the lawns of Lords, at least you had both options available). But then came Beefy Botham who would out-Aussie the Aussies by getting pissed, shagging barmaids and smashing their bowlers into various confectionery stalls and out again.

I was quite the sports tart back then and would enjoy anything which had a competitive edge to it. Red Rum was more than just pet food to me, John Curry and Torvill & Dean made ice skating exciting (I readily admit to crying when the row of 6.0s came up for Bolero), Maradona's Hand of God was not divine intervention just cheating (I cried again) and Borg vs McEnroe at Wimbledon gripped my imagination because, in those pre Tim Henman and Andy Murray days, we had no local heroes to get behind (though Virginia Wade gave a short-lived but rather more patriotic boost to the Queen's Silver Jubilee than the Sex Pistols had managed a few weeks before).

The Olympics were a nightmare during that period – terrorist attacks, corrupt officials, bankrupt host cities and so many national boycotts that it's amazing our policy of Swiss-like neutrality (which saw a GB team turn up every four years regardless of the political fall-out) didn't yield a greater tally of gold medals. The athletics was always good fun though. If Juantorena wasn't opening his legs and showing us his class then Daley Thompson was trying to whistle the national anthem and posh Seb Coe was taking on working class Steve Ovett in every running event the rules allowed them to enter, with World or Olympic records tumbling on almost every occasion (although the record breaker was only announced once Roy Castle and the McWhirter twins had officially endorsed the achievement).

I even watched snooker although I couldn't fathom how the game became so popular (other than the BBC using our licence fee to sell it back to us as hard as it could). We had plenty of ball games where people ran like the wind and battered each other senseless so why such a static one proved so popular is beyond me. I loved Alex Higgins and Jimmy White but 'hurricane' and 'whirlwind'?? Was this supposed to be ironic? They sauntered around a table with a stick, sometimes at a brisk walking pace I grant you, but it was hardly running the 100 metres in less than 10 seconds was it? And how on earth did Steve Boring Davis become the top TV personality of all of them? Snooker Loopy indeed.

My Dad and brother were very handy rugby players so I'd watch all the key Union games on telly (I've lost count how many times I'd seen the Baa Baas famous try vs the All Blacks in 1973 – "this is Gareth Edwards, a dramatic start, what a score" – until I married a kiwi and weirdly I've not seen it since). If I was lucky, Dad would take me to Twickenham. When Erica Roe turned up topless at the game against Australia in 1977, so did I (although, to be clear, I was 11 years old and we travelled to the match separately). I'd never seen my Dad so absorbed with what was happening on a rugby pitch as he was at the sight of a policeman's helmet cupping one of Erica's ample breasts and only just managing to fit it in.

Everyone could watch top sport on TV in those days because the main channels had all the popular events as well as the best presenters – Dickie Davies, Brian Moore, Jimmy 'Chinny Rec-kon' Hill and Frank

Bough (who lived down the road from me until recently and once, when I hummed the Grandstand theme tune to him as he walked past my house, hilariously told me – light entertainment legend that he was – to piss off). To be fair, we were lacking when it came to HD replays from 34 different camera angles but at least we didn't have VAR. Or Gary Lineker. The only time we saw him was slotting in the goals from three feet out rather than lecturing us on MOTD or social media. We didn't realise how lucky we were. He was famously the nation's favourite Mr Nice Guy because he never got sent off but, boy, has he been making up for it ever since.

Sport back then seems so different to today. Rugby players and footballers could act like Muhammad Ali (not the dancing feet or the rhyming couplets, I mean throwing punches) and not be reprimanded. Now they get sent off for a decent tackle. When the umpire gave you out, you were out and when the linesman raised his flag, it wasn't a goal. When a try was scored, the only person to see multiple replays of it was you at home while the ref got on with sorting out the conversion. You knew where you stood and could celebrate (or throw a tantrum like Keegan in Superstars) safe in the knowledge that the decision wouldn't be reversed. The fact that Kev got his bike race re-run is the exception which proves the rule.

Our commentators were equally reliable – if Dan Maskell exclaimed "oh I say", he invariably did and when Kenneth Wolstenholme told us they think it's all over, it was. The only reason we never saw the bowler holding the batsman's willy was because, sadly, TMS never actually suggested he was and it's an urban myth. And, if non-media savvy footballers and their managers gave an interview on MOTD or The Big Match, they told us what they actually thought rather than what their PR people told them they thought. As a result, you never quite knew what Brian Clough would say except if you lived in my house because then it would be my impression of him every night once I'd gone through my Frank Spencer and Dick Emery repertoire. Sport (and life) was so much simpler then.

25 FINDUS CRISPY PANCAKES

The absolute very first time I made Findus Crispy Pancakes was in the 80s. I was very proud of myself because it was the first food I actually cooked on my own. 40 years later, they would no doubt have remained my culinary pièce de résistance if the bastards at Findus still made the bloody things. Apparently, Birds Eye make them now 'with no artificial colours or flavours, new & tasty ingredients AND (their capitals not mine) with more filling.' It doesn't sound like they'll taste much like the originals anymore then.

My sister used to work for the Findus company when they were part of Nestlé and she gave me a few packets of ex-sales samples on my birthday (I was quite a bit younger than her and still am). They'd clearly defrosted a bit by the time I unwrapped them but my mum said they'd be fine to eat and not to be so ungrateful.

To be fair, my mum wasn't big on food safety and treated best before dates with a mixture of suspicion and mild amusement. Even as she got older and looked to pass on her wisdom to a new generation, she'd pull out dusty old cans of alphabetti spaghetti to feed my kids (her grandchildren), ignoring the fact that the best before dates had expired while their father was at college in the late 80s. She had the same approach with the equally dusty box of old toys which, as I've warned you in an earlier story, had been deliberately designed to endanger life (not by my mum, to be fair) and so were lead-painted, sharp-edged death trap equivalents of the salmonella-rich cans of pasta (which, even if they were inedible, at least gave my kids the opportunity of arranging the contents to spell the word 'boobs,' just like their old dad had done before them – so proud).

Findus Crispy Pancakes became a staple lunch for me and, inspired by our only celeb chef at the time, Fanny (may all your doughnuts look like Fanny's) Craddock, I began to experiment with accompaniments. There was obviously enough goodness in the pancakes themselves to mean I didn't need any veg but you could really bring them to life with some mashed … and, as all 70s/80s kids know, the only processed potato product available in those days was Smash. It took me quite a while to realise that it was actually potato. I assumed it was a tasty snack. It was made by Cadbury after all and they were sneakier bastards than Findus because they bombarded us with those addictive Martian adverts (voiced by Zippy of Rainbow – true story) specifically designed to make us badger mum to buy this fantastic sprinkling of chocolatey heaven … only to find out it was powdered potato. And with no social media to spread the news to less enlightened kids and their mums, they got away with it.

It's little surprise that this dry powder, even once you mixed it with hot water, tasted, well, dry and powdery. If you put a buttercup under its metaphorical chin, there's not much chance it would glow yellow. And, by the way, the clever scientists at Cambridge University have in recent years worked out that the strong reflective properties of the flower are down to epidermal layers designed to attract pollinators and nothing to do with whether you like butter or not. So, that's one more innocent children's game that can be consigned to the dustbin of playground history. At the same time, Oxford University scientists developed a vaccine for COVID. That's the positive impact of intense academic rivalry for you.

With mains sorted, the options for dessert were a little more limited. Gü hadn't been invented so Arctic roll was our special treat (we were given Angel Delight normally) but otherwise ice cream on sticks were only available in corner shops or from Mr Softee vans. You couldn't buy them in bulk from Gateway or Fine Fare and fish them out of your fridge whenever you felt like one. You had to travel to get a lolly and it was illegal in those days to eat one indoors. The only ice cream you had at home in your freezer were the tubs of vanilla which frosted over into clumps and tasted so sweet you'd gag. Just imagine if, like now, you could dip into your fridge whenever you liked to pick out a Fab or Funny Feet or Zoom or Mivvi or Count Dracula's Secret (black ice, red jelly ... absolute heaven). And, don't forget, you got a joke written on the stick too. Why were five and six terrified? Because seven ate nine. So, funny AND educational. They taught you to count though not necessarily to spell (I still write 8 as 'ate' to this day).

Purchase options for drinks were much the same but with one crucial difference. You still couldn't buy any of your favourite brands in the supermarket (except R Whites lemonade which was only a favourite because Elvis Costello's Dad – I'm not kidding – told you he was a secret lemonade-drinker) but you COULD get the exact Coke or Pepsi experience at home ... with a sodastream machine. And when I say 'exact' I clearly mean 'nothing like it.'

Sodastream drinks tasted truly awful. Like ice cream tubs, everything came out super-sweet. You never made one because you were thirsty or fancied a cool refreshing drink. You made it because you could pretend to be an evil scientist intent on poisoning the world – a case of fact and fiction colliding.

Most of the time though, my mum couldn't be doing with the palaver of the sodastream so, when she wanted me out of the house (which was every day during the holidays), she simply handed me juice drinks in cartons and a couple of packets of Smiths Salt 'n' Shake crisps (do you know anyone who didn't sprinkle the whole of the blue sachet into the bag – so what was the point of that then?) and packed me off to the playing fields with either a football if it was pouring with rain or, if it was just heavy drizzle, my cricket bat. Clearly I didn't play on my own so, Guy, Budgie, Chris & co, your mums were just as bad as mine.

In those days (except for the summer of 1976, yes even in Scotland) it always rained and so it was either irony or cruelty which drove drinks advertisers to sell their products to British audiences on the basis they were the perfect thirst quenchers for baking hot climates. My mum fell for it and either gave us Um Bongo which, according to Libbys, was extremely popular in the Congo or Kia Ora (maori for 'hello' so my NZ wife tells me) because it was adored by dog-impersonating crows in the Deep South of the USA (and, wow, wouldn't social media explode if the 'I'll be your dog' advert was aired today??).

And if you wanted something to tide you over between meals, a finger of fudge, as we all know, was just enough to give your kids a treat which, in practice, meant it was far too small to satisfy any growing young girl or boy but, on the plus side, its slogan kept a million of us occupied devising crude versions to sing about female teachers or your mate's mum.

Home economics was only taught in the girls school in my home town and there was no national culture of celebrity chefs to encourage us boys. In those days, Gordon Ramsey, Jamie Oliver and Hugh Fearnley-Whittingstall were sitting next to us in class, launching ink bombs with their rulers rather than encouraging us to cook (well, not Hugh perhaps – he was studying Latin at Eton) which just left Findus, with their crispy pancakes, and Fanny, with her unusually-shaped doughnuts, to inspire us in the kitchen.

26 XMAS NO.1s

The absolute very first time I remember hearing the Xmas No.1 in the singles chart and actually caring about who had made it to the top spot was in 1971 when my own purchase of Benny Hill's Ernie the Fastest Milkman had helped propel it to the No.1 position. The single sat proudly in my nascent record collection alongside the Sweet, Mud and Gary Glitter. I still have all these singles in my possession to this day (although I keep the Gary Glitter ones in a separate record box under lock and key for obvious reasons).

After this purchase and for a couple of golden decades to come, the name of every Xmas No.1 is as indelibly etched in my memory as each winner of the FA Cup over the same time period. After around 1990 though, along with most of the country, I stopped paying much attention to either.

The Xmas No.1s in the 60s were predictably dominated by the Beatles but the 70s opened up an incredibly eclectic run of seasonal chart-toppers right through to the 90s when the influx of girl/boy bands (Spice Girls, Westlife, Girls Aloud) and Simon Cowell's X-Factor PR juggernaut sucked the joy out of Xmas and redesigned it on the basis of corporate greed and self-interest (much like football's brief flirtation with the European Super League but a lot more expertly masterminded).

Over the 70s & 80s, we got an unbelievable mix of all-time classics, Xmas anthems and novelty pap. And Cliff Richard. Here are all of them in order from Ernie in 1971:

- Ernie – Benny Hill (vs Two Ton Ted from Teddington who drove the baker's van and also implored us to tell mummy about the honey in the Sugar Puffs TV ads).
- Long Haired Lover – Little Jimmy Osmond (another flipping Osmond. They'll discover a girl in the family next!! What? Oh, apparently they managed to rustle one up the following year).
- Merry Xmas Everybody – Slade (this one has rounded off every Xmas office party ever since to provide Noddy and the boys with a reliably large annuity).
- Lonely This Xmas – Mud (and, much to their annoyance, this one hasn't).
- Bohemian Rhapsody – Queen (classic No.1).
- When a Child is Born – Johnny Mathis (carrying Cliff's torch while he was on sabbatical ... and you'll notice that phrase symbolically includes the letters 'ffs').

- Mull of Kintyre – Wings (classic No.2).
- Mary's Boy Child – Boney M (a hastily-released cover to cash in on the group's popularity: they could do no wrong in the 70s … partly because half of the band weren't allowed to take part in the recordings owing to the minor inconvenience of not actually being able to sing).
- Another Brick in the Wall – Pink Floyd (classic No.3).

That's probably the perfect cross-section of Xmas hits – three absolute classics, a few seasonal sing-a-longs/tear-jerkers and a couple of novelty numbers.

The 80s were much the same:

- There's No One Quite Like Grandma – St Winifred's School Choir (my granny had dementia by then so let's hope, for other people's sake, that the kids at St Winifred's had got it right).
- Don't You Want Me – Human League (has anyone seen the version which simply repeats the line 'working as a waitress in a cocktail bar' throughout the whole song? It's weirdly addictive. Just type the lyric into YouTube and look for the upload by SanderVidNL).
- Save Your Love – Renée and Renato (tell me this never happened and it wasn't written by the bloke who voiced Metal Mickey. Nope, it did and it was).
- Only You – Flying Pickets (a Yazoo cover but I have to admit to loving this version, especially the scary bald bloke who you assume would belt out the bass notes before beating you up but instead sings falsetto and probably loves Eurovision).
- Do They Know its Xmas – Band Aid (one hit wonders).
- Merry Xmas Everybody – Shakin Stevens (the spirit of Slade channelled via the Welsh Elvis … if Elvis had shot to fame on the US

equivalent of Cheggers Plays Pop and chosen to sing about property development (if it wasn't ole houses, it was green doors) rather than whatever colour of suede shoes he happened to be wearing).

- Reet Petite – Jackie Wilson (great song – do you remember the BBC's plasticene animation film which propelled it back into the charts?)
- Always on My Mind – Pet Shop Boys (good song but it's just a cover and it kept the Pogues' Fairytale of New York off the top).
- Mistletoe & Wine – Cliff Richard (there's the bastard – I knew he'd be in here somewhere).
- Do They Know its Xmas – Band Aid II (beating Last Xmas by Wham but with a second-rate line-up compared to the original ... chiefly because of Cliff's involvement – and spot the 'ffs' again).

Cliff hit the top again in 1990 with the lamentable Saviour's Day but, despite my memories of countless seasonal chart-toppers, he never actually achieved another Xmas No.1 (although Millennium Prayer was top of the charts in 1999 leading up to Xmas Day itself but lost out on a technicality ... and that technicality being that normal recording-buying people eventually decided they didn't actually like it very much).

After that, the Xmas charts lost all their pizzazz with only Mr Blobby and Bob The Builder, in 1993 and 2000, reminding us that Brits are prone to losing all critical music faculties at that time of year and wasting their money on the stupidest of stuff.

The real problem for me is the X-Factor years of the mid/late noughties. I loved it when you genuinely didn't know which single would get to No.1 but you had confidence (possibly misplaced, I know) that whichever song made it to the top spot would secure it on merit. Simon Cowell's run of Xmas No.1s just felt so cynical and calculated – the result of a business strategic plan rather than a wacky races-style starting line-up of classic/silly/Xmassy tunes, one of which would happen to tug on the collective heartstrings of the British public sufficiently to come out on top. Five No.1s in six years for Cowell I think – I don't know for certain because these five are the only names I've failed to recognise on the list so I assume they're the one-hit wonders which the X-Factor PR machine pumped to the top of the charts and then dumped back to instant obscurity again.

I like and fully support the Rage Against the Machine fightback as the fly in that six year ointment but it's really just another example of manipulation (much like Ladbaby). Don't get me wrong, I far prefer it to whatever the media juggernauts were pushing at the time but it still seems to deny the record-buying/streaming public a No.1 chosen simply on the basis of whether they liked the tune or not. Not everything needs to be a protest or a signal of undoubted virtue. Sometimes it can be spontaneous and uncalculated. Sometimes it can just be Mr Blobby. Sorry, forget I ever said that.

My copy of Benny Hill's Ernie: this is the original one I owned and not one of the many pieces of memorabilia I've bought off eBay for huge sums of money in recent years to replace the stuff my mum threw away. I know the kids missed out on a good education as a result but they'll thank me one day (although granny might stay in the doghouse a while longer).

THINGS WE WISH WE HAD BACK THEN

Part One: Mobile Phones

How on earth did we survive without mobile phones? Well, we did and, let's be honest, it didn't seem too tough, did it? Our parents never knew where we were half the time and weren't that bothered either. They'd lived through the war as kids after all so were hardly going to worry about us falling off the merry-go-round and scraping our knee.

If we wanted a chat, we went round to someone's house – we found it a more reliable way of expressing our feelings than using emojis. We took photos on our Kodak Instamatics but rarely of our genitals and, on the odd occasion we might've done (and I'm admitting to nothing), it would never have occurred to us to send them to anyone else. Also, Truprint would've probably refused to post them back to us anyway.

I know it's convenient to have your entire record & video collection in your pocket but how much fun was it to go through the elaborate (and sometime torturous) ritual of playing vinyl, tapes or video cassettes? "Lots" is the answer before you say anything to the contrary.

And finally, without mobile phones, we'd never have invented that quaint ritual of talking to each other round the dinner table instead of watching cat videos on YouTube. That said, most of our suppers ended in family rows and some of those cat videos are genuinely hilarious so I suppose it's swings & roundabouts really.

27 NOT THE NINE O'CLOCK NEWS

The absolute very first time I watched Not the Nine O'Clock News was near the end of the 1st series in 1979. I'm not sure how or why I didn't see the first few episodes – as I keep on reminding you, there was bugger all to watch on telly at the time so anything half decent was difficult to miss – but, to be fair, Sapphire & Steel was on ITV just beforehand with the young Joanna Lumley so I'd probably gone to my bedroom for a lie-down.

The 1st series of NTNOCN met with mixed reviews but the 2nd series took off when Griff Rhys Jones replaced Chris Langham (later of the Thick Of It and child pornography fame) in the line-up. Griff was not a major star (that accolade went to Rowan Atkinson and, by god, didn't he just know it) but Griff was the classic hard-working journeyman who provides the heartbeat to any team – the under-rated holding midfielder in a football side or the bassist standing at the back of the band. No offence to Griff (or Mel), though, but we just wanted to see Rowan and Pamela Stephenson, especially when she opened her blouse in the American Express parody advert and asked us whether we'd like to rub her tits too, putting the pause/rewind functions of a million VCRs to the ultimate test.

After just four series and 27 episodes (how on earth have we managed to stomach over 60 series and 500 episodes of Have I Got News For You?), the show was brought to an end by a combination of Rowan Atkinson, his publicist and his ego. When the production team and cast were meeting up to discuss taking NTNOCN to the next level, with aspirations of movies and breaking America, Atkinson cheerily announced over dinner that, despite the group being 'very nice people', his agent had told him 'not to play with the 2nd XI anymore' and, with that, he left the restaurant and the show – a team player of David Brent proportions. And for those of you who love Mr Bean, poor Rowan was recently quoted as finding the character 'stressful and exhausting' and he 'looks forward to the end of it'. So that's a thanks for all the support then.

Not to kick the boot in (although why not, he's a global megastar so won't give a damn what I have to say) but a year or so before his sensitively-pitched resignation speech, he had offered to edit a 90 minute video to showcase the best bits of each NTNOCN series. Apparently the first draft he showed to the producer, John Lloyd (no, not the tennis player who married Chris Evert and so paved the way for Guy Ritchie, Chris Martin and the artist formerly known as Prince Harry to shack up with

US celeb royalty), was basically a Rowan Atkinson highlights package which included absolutely no footage of Pamela Stephenson at all. His initial response was mild surprise, as though he hadn't actually noticed this omission, but, when pressed by Lloyd, he conceded that he "never really thought she was that funny anyway".

In the early 70s, when I wasn't practising Gary Glitter impressions in front of the mirror (by which, for the avoidance of doubt, I mean pretending to sing his hits), I was learning all the Monty Python tunes from the albums we had at home (I had older siblings). I could recite the Bruce's Philosopher song in full and therefore I did so fairly often to family, friends and, on one occasion, my choirmaster ('there's nothing Nietzsche couldn't teach yer 'bout the raising of the wrist, Socrates himself was permanently pissed'). It taught me all I ever needed to know about philosophy, excessive drinking and Australians. I'm not sure what the choirmaster learned from it but he kept on looking at me with a leer on his face and so he obviously enjoyed the song too.

NTNOCN took the song-writing to the next level. They may have been parodies of popular musical genres & performers but many were great songs in their own right and, much like the Pythons, filled with clever lyrics and masterful rhymes. Unlike the Pythons though, they reflected music which was currently in the charts. From Kate Bush's 'you're all trying hard to get inside my leotard' to the Two Tone I Like Bouncing song ('that doesn't need announcing judging by the way your balls are bouncing') and the Mosley-inspired 'although I cannot claim to be any great authority, as far as I'm concerned the sun shone out of his oratory'. After Grease, I was a big ONJ fan so I loved the 'Bloody Typical' song about how her lack of bedroom action meant she was looking for a young man in a rogering situation … and, as far as my adolescent self was concerned, my home town was surely as good a place for her to search as any.

One classic sketch was Life of Python about our lord John Cleese which was a reminder of how large a shadow Monty Python cast over every sketch show which succeeded them in the 70s & 80s. They were the

Godfathers of comedy but even they presented their women as either token totty (à la Dick Emery and Benny Hill) or battle-axes in drag. It was Terry Jones who got to tell us that Brian was a very naughty boy and not actually the Messiah, leaving Thora Hird and Mollie Sugden to work out how their auditions had gone so badly wrong.

In contrast the roles which Pamela Stephenson adopted in NTNOCN were on a par with her fellow performers (except Rowan obviously). I loved how her newsreaders exaggerated the pronunciation of the foreign names and that her barely-intelligible Janet Street Porter asked Glaswegian husband-to-be, Billy Connelly, if people found him difficult to understand. My favourite was her social worker ("I know these kids, um, I've worked with them") when she weighed in on a heated but erudite debate about hooliganism and concluded that the solution was almost certainly to cut off their goolies.

The writing team were mainly in-house but the Constable Savage sketch was sent in to the show by a police forensic scientist who never had anything else published in his life (one of the better one-hit wonders in a peer group which admittedly includes Joe Dolce's Shaddap You Face). Richard Curtis, one of the principal writers, was a mate of Atkinson's from Uni and knew which side his bread was buttered so stuck with the rubbery-faced comedian at the end of NTNOCN, firstly making his name on Blackadder and then encouraging Hugh Grant to steal our hearts in Four Weddings and a Funeral. Unfortunately, he felt this gave him the mandate to inflict Notting Hill (not totally awful) and Love Actually (totally awful) on a compliant British public.

My favourite sketch though has always been the Swedish Chemist Shop where Mel Smith asks for deodorant in a heavy Scandinavian accent, Rowan the shopkeeper replies, in equally-thick intonation, "ball or aerosol?" before Mel ends with the classic "neither, I want it for my armpits". They both turn to the camera with a slightly apologetic look although I'm sure I can spot a glint of jealous fury in Atkinson's eye that Mel was given the punchline instead of him.

28 WATCH WITH MOTHER

The absolute very first programme I saw on BBC's Watch With Mother series was probably the Flower Pot Men which was the forerunner of Teletubbies and In The Night Garden and equally dreadful at teaching kids to speak. Bill & Ben spouted such mumbo jumbo that 'flobbadob' and 'weeeeed' were all I came out with at kindergarten while the other kids, no doubt weaned on the Open University by proper parents, recited their times tables instead.

It was meant to be educational but seemed more like the BBC guide to snitching. In every episode, Little Weed (the manipulative bitch) would encourage us to pin the blame for some horticultural calamity on one of the characters – was it Bill or was it Ben? – and whoever we fingered would be marched off to some correctional facility by the copper off Andy Pandy. I always suspected the perpetrator was actually Weed herself but she was like H in Line of Duty and seemed to slip through the net every time.

Besides Flower Pot Men and Andy Pandy, the other Watch With Mother programmes I was plonked in front of were Camberwick Green and Trumpton. I'm pretty sure I didn't actually enjoy any of these shows because I remember finding all of them absolutely terrifying. I honestly mean that. The opening of Camberwick Green (ie Junior Wicker Man) showed a musical box being wound up by a clown (and we all know how evil those bastards are) to summon one of the other puppets to slowly emerge from the depths of Hades. The only welcome source of light relief was Windy Miller whose name became so closely associated with farting that my kids have actually heard the expression despite never seeing the programme it was lifted from.

Apparently, at the end of the series, it was reported that the creator of the puppets had them all cremated in his back garden because he came to the conclusion that they wouldn't be worth anything in the future. I beg to differ on both counts. I know for a fact that there are several survivors because I have bought half a dozen of the originals off eBay for sizeable sums of money (I see it as an investment) from some very nice collectors in Eastern Europe (they tell me the show was extremely popular over there). Am I not a businessman of truly Del-Boy calibre? Chateauneuf du Pape I am.

Trumpton was less scary admittedly but so weird that the League of Gentlemen must have based Royston Vasey's village on it ('a local shop for local people' and all that). It had an odd variety of tradesmen, including a bloke who mended wooden benches (Chippy Minton), a window cleaner who doubled as a chimney sweep (Mr Robinson) and a fire brigade (yes, you know all the names) who never seemed to attend any fires but still managed to enjoy gainful employment rescuing anything which required an unusually-long ladder to reach it.

I can't remember what I found terrifying about Looby Loo in Andy Pandy but I felt the same about Jemima on Play School so I expect this explains my anxiety issues with the opposite sex which would no doubt be recognised by all my former girlfriends (by which I mean both of them … namely, my wife and a girl called Miranda from primary school).

I was obviously a timid and insecure little chap because, as I've admitted previously, I was also terrified of the arched window in Play School and that devil-doll, Hamble. Brian Cant, on the other hand, was a reassuring avuncular figure who … oh no, don't tell me, has he been cancelled now too?

Watch With Mother was, in today's language, the umbrella brand for kids TV and had been since the 1950s. It was oddly-named, at least in my household, because my mum used it as a babysitting service while she poured herself a gin and tonic in the other room. Also, what a formal title! Nothing warm & cuddly from the BBC like Watch with Mummy. I know the Beeb wants to be seen as young and trendy nowadays (it would be called 'Watch with Mother & Mother' if it was aired today) but, to my generation, it will always be Auntie … and, in the case of kids telly in the 70s, a miserable old child-hating one at that.

I don't remember listening to the radio much at home but I've got a feeling that some bored or hungover primary school teacher (either Miss M or Miss K – they were sisters) might have switched on the radio version of Watch With Mother to keep the class entertained when they couldn't be bothered to. Imaginatively-titled 'Listen With Mother', the programme started with the classic "Are you sitting comfortably? Then I'll begin". This was usually the cue for Miss K (or Miss M) to fall asleep or sneak off to the toilet and for us to stop sitting comfortably and start throwing rubbers, pencil sharpeners and chalk across the classroom instead. By the way, you won't find any of those things in schools anymore so what on earth do kids tend to throw at each other today? Just on-line abuse, I suppose.

Jackanory was the programme we graduated onto after we'd watched or listened with (or, in my case, without) mother. I just checked the narrators in the early 70s and it was an incredible collection of British acting talent, presumably filling in between jobs. We had stage royalty in Helen Mirren, Judi Dench and Martin Jarvis, the officers in Dad's Army (not the troops obviously), Indiana Jones' boss, a couple of Doctor Who's, both Likely Lads, Carry On regulars like Bernard Cribbens & Kenneth Williams and member of parliament, famous grandson and petfood advertiser, Clement Freud.

You could tell the really big stars. The more successful they were, the less they needed the Jackanory appearance money and so only presented the show for a few weeks (like Helen Mirren and Judi Dench). Bernard Cribbens, on the other hand, must have been going through a really long dip in his career because he kept on turning up to read to us. I guess The Wombles was only a part-time gig and didn't pay particularly well. Careers were long in those days, partly because you couldn't write off-colour tweets likely to be dug up 20 years later by some saddo intent on getting you fired from your job. I bet old Bernard would have been a prime candidate for that if the technology had existed.

And then, overnight, you'd moved on from Jackanory and your innocence was gone. You started to watch the Sweeney and called everyone (even your mum) a toilet. You didn't believe in Father Christmas or the Tooth Fairy anymore (you never believed in the Easter Bunny in the first place but you laughed at the American kids who did). You found a job, got married, had kids and began to watch out for mother rather than watch with her. And now, with bad backs, piles and pot stomachs, you've completely forgotten what it's like to sit comfortably but don't seem to have quite as much trouble remembering who Windy Miller is. How I miss the old days.

29 WACKY RACES

The absolute very first time I saw Wacky Races would've been the early 70s I guess. It wasn't a series which you followed with bated breath. It just seemed to be on telly all the time when I was younger. Do you know how many episodes there were? Seventeen. Yep, one seven. I wouldn't say the format was formulaic but we must've watched them over & over again without realising it. It's all relative though – Roadrunner was simply the same episode repeated 40-odd times.

I've banged on previously how fantastic cartoon theme tunes were in the old days but I hardly remember the Wacky Races one at all. I've found a Peugeot advert which used it along with live action versions of the characters. Not sure if I like the idea but pop a combination of those words into YouTube and see what you think.

There were two races per episode and 11 cars with the top three shown on the podium at the end. I always thought Penelope Pitstop was the most successful contestant but apparently the Slag Brothers (oh how I wish I knew the cavemen were called that when I was younger) had the most podium finishes. Dick Dastardly & Muttley, predictably, were the only drivers never to win it. They did actually come first once but were denied the victory we were all secretly craving by a slow-motion replay which saw our initial euphoria snuffed out in the cruellest of fashion … sound familiar, football fans?

Here's a rundown of the runners and riders:

00 Mean Machine – Dick Dastardly and Muttley in a car which looked suspiciously like a rip-off of the Batmobile. These two were the stand-out stars of the show who, like the lead singers of the best bands (Sting, Annie Lennox, and, er, Limahl), were always destined to go solo in their own series. They clearly had the fastest car and always took an early lead but then made the schoolboy error of stopping to sabotage their competitors. Why on earth didn't they just drive on at a leisurely pace and win the race?! Drat and double drat.

01 Boulder Mobile – The Slag Brothers aka Rock & Gravel. They sounded like that drunken Paul Whitehouse character who speaks a load of gibberish punctuated by the odd coherent expression. Suffering a breakdown in the mountains, it always seemed an advantage to be driving a car made out of rocks given the ready availability of spare parts on offer. I loved them hitting each other over the heads with clubs. I just find gratuitous violence funny sometimes.

02 Creepy Coupe – The Gruesome Twosome. This is what my mum used to call me and any friend I invited round. They never came back twice. A Munsters-style spooky vehicle complete with permanent raincloud and dragon in the bell tower (bats, yes, but dragons?). I always had a soft spot for these two. They barely won though, possibly as a direct result.

03 Convert-a-car – Professor Pat Pending, inventor. More like a magician with a boat-like car which could mutate into various other vehicles (and you wondered where the idea for Transformers came from?). I always felt he didn't look much like a Pat. The only one I knew was Irish and played in goal for Spurs so perhaps I wasn't the best judge.

04 Crimson Haybaler – Red Max. Missed out on the baddie role with only himself to blame – you need a proper villain name like Dick Dastardly or Sylvester 'Hooded Claw' Sneekly and 'Red Max' simply wasn't going to cut the mustard. As a result, he hardly ever appeared in the show. In fact, I had to re-watch a couple of episodes to prove to myself he even existed. He had a plane but, for some inexplicable reason, raced on the road which rather blunted his competitive advantage. Absolute muppet … and, if I had to narrow it down, probably the Swedish chef.

05 Compact Pussycat (really??) – Penelope Pitstop. This was in the pre-Hooded Claw days ("hel-up, hel-up, it's the Hooded Clor-wer" which, after binge-watching numerous episodes on YouTube, I'm pretty sure she never actually said) and well before Frankie Goes to Hollywood promised to protect us from him (er, why – it was a beautiful Xmas ballad not a novelty song?). She seemed more interested in her make-up than the race – an odd concern in the middle of an endurance rally – and was my first schoolboy crush, sandwiched between Looby Loo and the toon with the big tits in Who Framed Roger Rabbit.

06 Army Surplus Special – Sergeant Blast & Private Meekley in their tank. I didn't actually know what 'army surplus' meant in my younger days but I assumed the US military was full and these two couldn't get in. Not my favourites and the fact they were the least successful racers bar DD&M suggests I wasn't alone. The only soldiers I'd come across were on Dad's Army or in my Action Man collection so I didn't have many positive role models to draw from.

07 Bulletproof Bomb – The Ant Hill Mob. These lot were small and needed a shave. They were a strange take on the Seven Dwarves with Penelope as their Snow White damsel in distress. I always enjoyed them sticking their feet through the bottom of the chassis when their motor packed up.

08 Arkansas Chuggabug – Lazy Luke & Blubber Bear (who looked like a Yogi rip-off). I wasn't a big fan of hillbillies (and I hadn't even watched Deliverance by then) but I grew fonder of them once I'd been introduced to Daisy Dook off Dukes of Hazzard. I quite liked the old guy using his bare feet to steer and I vaguely remember a squirrel in the engine. Either that or the space dust I was liberally consuming at the time was far more hallucinogenic than I thought.

09 Turbo Terrific – Peter Perfect – I remembered him being a bit full of himself but he was actually just the perfect gentleman (a bit like Harry Enfield's Tim 'Nice but Dim'), full of chivalrous gestures which tended to backfire. He definitely wanted to shag 'Pretty Penny' and so was effectively my rival which clearly made him a sex pest. I loved it when he lost.

10 Buzz Wagon – Rufus Ruffcut & Sawtooth, a lumberjack & beaver combination and the man/beast counterpart to DD&M but without the same chemistry (the beaver didn't even snigger). Rufus looked like Desperate Dan off the Dandy and, if he had the same love for meaty pies, I suspect his chubby-cheeked little companion was living on borrowed time.

So, they you are. I know I said at the beginning that this wasn't a series which you avidly looked forward to but, watching some old episodes again, I was surprised how well I knew the characters and how much I liked them. One in particular. When I was young, I always wondered what Penelope Pitstop would look like in her bra and pants and I'd get a tingly feeling as a result. Come to think of it, it's crossed my mind quite a few times since over the years with a very similar result. I've even got a picture of her tucked away in my underpants drawer … at least I did until my wife found it recently. Curses, foiled again.

30 DOCTOR WHO

The absolute very first time I watched Doctor Who was with Jon Pertwee in the 1970s (well, not *with* him – he was the one on telly). They say you can tell someone's age by their favourite Doctor and mine were the suave silver fox and Tom Baker, the nutter with the scarf and the jelly babies (although I was also fond of Matt Smith but that would make me c.10 years old). JP must have been distraught when he found out he was regenerating into a buffoon but he turned into a scarecrow himself a few months later so be careful what you wish for.

I love how JP epitomised his era – frilly shirts, velvet smoking jackets and capes – a combination of late 60s Kinks, early 70s prog rock and Liberace. TB, on the other hand, was timeless (yes I know, literally), meaning there was no era where his car crash of fashion styles (and I use that term loosely) would feel at home. I thought he looked pretty cool to be honest but I was a big fan of tank tops at the time so probably not the best one to judge.

I never missed an episode when I was younger. You couldn't afford to. Not only were VCRs yet to be invented but BBC producers were so cost-conscious that they wiped the tapes two minutes after broadcast so that they could reuse them and save licence payers' hard-earned money. How things change.

Even when I was poorly (that's what our mums called 'being ill' in the old days), I'd watch the latest episode lying on the couch with a big orange bottle of lucozade – in the 70s the advertisers told us to drink it when we were sick in bed rather than halfway through the cycling leg of a triathlon – and some tablets which looked like spangles with the dent in the middle but didn't taste quite as nice. If that didn't perk me up, the threat of castor oil and my older brother rubbing Vicks on my chest invariably did the trick.

In the 70s, the BBC was focussed on making quality programmes (I know, who'd have thought it?) and left magazines & merchandising to others. They published the Radio Times though and the Xmas bumper issue was the family bible for festive viewing. We were all allowed to mark our preferred options with an asterisk but clashes fell in favour of mum & dad who tended to forget that Xmas was meant to be a time for children. So did the Beeb too because Doctor Who Xmas Specials, at that stage, were but a glint in the eye of Russell T. Davies and he was only our age so not much use to us really.

In terms of merchandising, Palitoy managed the Doctor Who catalogue. I would have killed for the K9 toy they brought out in the late 70s. It said "affirmative, master" when you pressed the button! Back then, parents steadfastly refused to buy us anything expensive for birthdays and Xmas no matter how much we tried to guilt-trip them. I was lucky enough to catch mumps one winter and, as a result, the action man commando with realistic hair and gripping hands was underneath the tree. It would have needed to be smallpox for them to put K9 in my stocking though.

I always felt Doctor Who was the scariest show on telly. When the sea devils emerged onto the beach (on the Isle of Wight for some reason), you really did hide behind the settee and, even when the cybermen sported crap helmets made out of cloth and silver foil, like something Valerie Singleton had shown you how to make on Blue Peter, they still managed to give you nightmares later on, even if they didn't threaten to 'delete' you in those days.

That said, you really shat your pants when the Public Information Films came on. As you know, I've clearly been scarred by these. They were truly terrifying – kids being drowned by Donald 'Grim Reaper' Pleasence or electrocuted trying to retrieve their frisbees or being mangled on motorbikes under the wheels of a Ford Cortina to force our parents to think once, think twice, think BIKE (cue karate chop). Jon Pertwee himself got the Green Cross Code gig ahead of Darth Vader and tried to teach us road safety with a bizarre acronym called SPLINK which was so complicated and convoluted that we'd have crashed through the windscreen of an Austin Allegro before we'd reached the letter 'L.'

After Tom Baker left in the early 80s, the show slowly went downhill and was taken off air altogether in 1989 until its revival in 2005. In the innocent days of those first few series, we hadn't worked out that Doctor Who may not have been his real name or that you could escape the daleks by walking up some stairs so I must admit to loving Russell's reboot of the series (as well as his Xmas Specials) when he referenced most of the things we enjoyed about the show in our youth and wove them into the new stories.

Production values were improved too. In our day, special effects weren't particularly special and gizmos looked like they'd been borrowed from the set of Tomorrow's World (the ending of which most of us watched every Thursday because it was on just before Top of the Pops).

The new series gave me a chance to introduce the scariest programme on TV to my kids who, having been weaned on Alien vs Predator, would simply snigger at how unrealistic and tame the Daleks & Cybermen were while I took up my customary position behind the settee. I had the last laugh though when the Weeping Angels turned up and scared the shit out of them. They're both grown-up now and tell me that the experience traumatised them for years but at least I got to prove my point so it was obviously worth it.

Once I'd got them hooked and we'd all sit round the TV as a family to watch the show like we used to do in the old days, the bastards at the BBC decided it would be a good idea to stop entertaining us & start lecturing us instead and we all lost interest again. Kids have got their teachers and parents to advise them about the moral standards they should set themselves. They hardly want or need a TV programme based on a thousand year old time-travelling alien to do it as well.

In the Beeb's desperate quest for diversity and moral re-education, it seems to have forgotten that the most important aspect of Doctor Who, and indeed any entertainment show on TV, is to come up with wonderful stories which excite, intrigue and amaze the viewer. That's what they used to do – naively, crudely and without today's polish and clever wit perhaps ... but without much of an agenda either. We really don't care what sex or colour the Doctor and his/her companions are so we're a bit non-plussed why this should form a central plank of every single storyline while presenting us with a decolonised re-writing of history which none of us actually asked for.

I assume I'm straying into hate crime territory here and I guess it's at this point that I'm supposed to apologise for my privilege and promise to re-educate myself in order to change for the better. But, as Elton John once said to me (and the rest of the TOTP audience), sorry seems to be the hardest word and I just don't think I can give an apology the sincerity it deserves. Expect my facebook page, in true cybermen style, to get deleted any day soon.

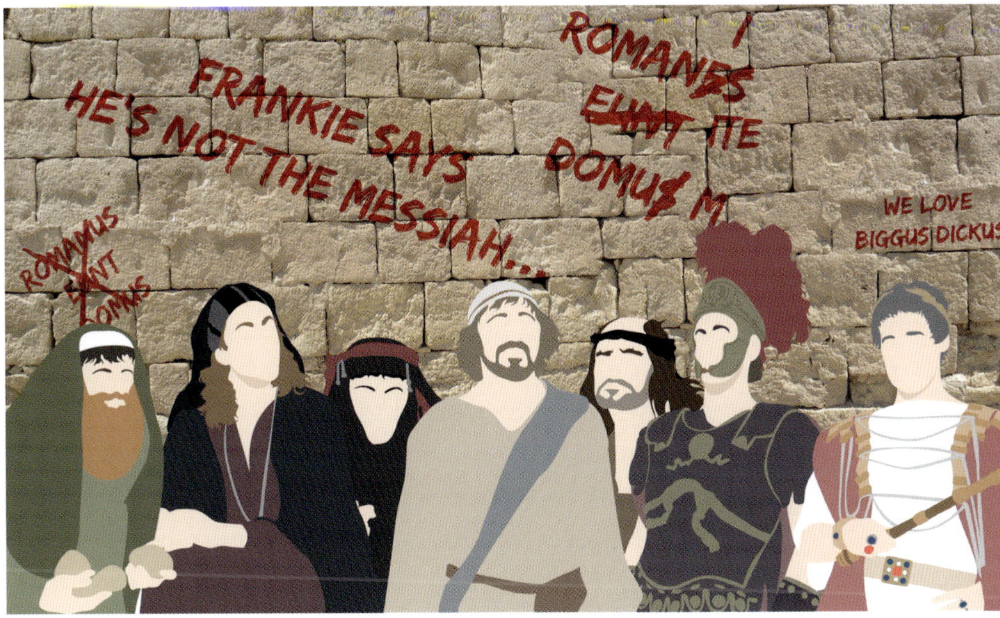

31 LIFE OF BRIAN

The absolute very first time I saw Life of Brian was when it hit the cinema in 1979. A few years earlier, Monty Python had been kind enough to fart in our general direction, introduce us to some knights which said 'Ni' and dismiss the loss of limbs in combat as mere flesh wounds but, by the time the decade was drawing to a close, we were in need of a follow-up to the Holy Grail for some fresh quotes to shout across the classroom before the teacher turned up (or afterwards as well if it was Squibby Bowman).

The Pythons had played pretty fast and loose with the Arthurian legend – I'm pretty sure they completely made up the killer rabbit episode for instance – so we didn't expect them to stay quite as faithful as they did to the story of Christ, lifting much of the material from the same source used by Tim Rice and Andrew Lloyd-Webber for Jesus Christ Superstar who, as all schoolchildren at the time knew, wore frilly knickers and a playtex bra (an aspect of his life which the Pythons, respectfully, decided to leave out of their biopic).

This omission clearly wasn't sufficient to stave off the controversy which threatened to derail the project, particularly when the original backers, EMI, pulled out just before production started. They had form in this regard and had similarly got cold feet a couple of years earlier when the Sex Pistols called Bill Grundy a dirty fucker on Thames TV. That got you sacked in the 70s – they'd call it a PR coup nowadays and no one would bat an eyelid. Instead, ex-Beatle and famous zebra-crosser George Harrison raided his piggy bank (do these still exist or are they just virtual nowadays?) and stepped in with the £2m funding on the basis that he loved the idea and just wanted to be able to see the film, making it, as Eric Idle pointed out, the most expensive cinema ticket in history. He was also given a cameo role as a thank you but proved to be a better guitarist than actor because his one line, "ullo", had to be redubbed by Michael Palin in post-production.

Grown-ups in Christian communities across the globe got their knickers in a twist about Life of Brian but, as kids, we weren't particularly bothered about the blasphemy debate. We were pretty clear that it was just a parody and that Brian was not literally intended to represent the Son of God but then we were teenagers so what did we know? I remember telling my mates at school that it seemed an obvious satire on organised religion and the mass credulity engendered by social conformism and group-think. I was 13 at the time and they bog-washed me straight afterwards which seemed a fairly accurate reflection of the level of debate going on in the media back then too.

Despite the religious furore ignited by the film, there were only two topics which the nation's youth wanted to discuss at school: speech impediments and full-frontal nudity. In the 70s and early 80s, before it was made a hate crime, we were allowed by law to take the piss out of how people talked and so the Pythons took full advantage by not only targeting lisps (Bigguth Dickuth) but also rhotacism (which, as any school kid can tell you, is a problem with the letter 'r'). Our favourite speech-impeded line from the film was "he wanks very highly in Wome" which we found even funnier than writing 'shelloil', or even more hilariously, 'boobies' upside down on our calculators.

On top of that, the film had not one but two scenes of full-frontal nudity. Don't forget, this was before your average ten year old could watch hardcore porn on their smart phones during maths. We didn't even see our parents in the nuddy because they would undress in the dark and only emerge from the bedroom if they had their jim jams on (unlike me nowadays, going commando as I lounge in my chair downstairs like Sharon Stone in Basic Instinct). So, it was quite an experience for us to see Graham Chapman, as Brian, showing us his willy before his girlfriend, Judith, flashed her pubes (and when I say 'flashed', I mean 'permanently kept on screen for several seconds') which happened to be the sexiest thing I'd seen on screen since Charlie's Angels (all three of them) played strip poker with Bosley in the agency office. What? That wasn't actually a scene in the series? Hmmm, wonder where I saw that one then.

We Brits have always tended to like our comedians to be well-educated as well as funny and Oxbridge has churned out its fair share, including all of the Goodies, three quarters of Not the Nine O'Clock News, both of Fry and Laurie and the full UK contingent of Pythons. As a result, Life of Brian had a strong educational element to it. The list of things the Romans had done for us proved a far better history lesson than the ones we had to sit through at school (although the brilliantly-named Bartle Frere did his best to liven things up for us) and the Roman centurion's corrections to Brian's graffiti made me understand Latin grammar rules for the first (and last) time.

Life of Brian seems to have aged pretty well. I asked my grown-up kids whether their friends would appreciate Monty Python and was given the thumbs up (on a text of course – we don't actually speak). My kids themselves don't count because I force-fed them a constant diet of 70s/80s nostalgia during their formative years but theirs is a generation which was largely born this century and so thinks Grease is a country in Southern Europe, TV is something you watch when you've lost your iPhone and space dust ought to be cleaned up with a Dyson.

That said, 40-50 years on, only Michael Palin has kept his place with the public as a national treasure. John Cleese was clearly the most talented and his subsequent output – especially Fawlty Towers – cements his place at the top of the tree but he's grown increasingly irascible as he's got older (haven't we all?) and his refusal to bow to the social media liberal elite has seen him sent to the Twitter naughty corner more than once in recent years.

Of the others, Eric Idle made an unlikely sandwich in the London 2012 Olympic closing ceremony between ELO & Muse and the rest are either American or dead (no more, ceased to be, kicked the bucket, run down the curtain and joined the choir invisible etc). After Life of Brian, I'm not sure what sort of reception they'd have received from the Great Film Director in the Sky (who, if he actually exists, hopefully looks like one of Terry Gilliam's animations and has a wicked sense of humour … well, not wicked obviously).

God: If you want to come in here, you have to really hate the Romans

Graham Chapman: I do

God: Oh yeah, how much?

GC: A lot!

God: Right, you're in

Cut to Chapman and Jesus at the Pearly Gates, leading the heavenly choir in a sing-a-long of 'always look on the bright side of life' while Terry Jones tells them off for being very naughty boys.

Just as hilarious today as it always used to be.

32 BOARD GAMES

The absolute very first time I played a board game was probably Totopoly (the horse racing one) in the early 70s. As the youngest in the family, I decided it was my job to move the plastic figures (not just mine but anyone's who was playing) and had a tendency to snap them in my excitement. This particularly annoyed my Dad because he knew he'd have a fiddly repair job on his hands and the poor horse would end up with blobs of UHU on its hooves. He told me that this was how you mended racehorses with broken legs in the real world but I'd watched the Grand National and knew that a refusal at Becher's Brook and the merest hint of a turned ankle would have the stewards reaching for the bolt gun.

In contrast, the paraphernalia and parts which came with Monopoly and Cluedo were virtually indestructible … so I lost them instead. We can't be the only family today who have hand-me-down sets where the Monopoly top hat has been replaced with a Subbuteo figure or a frayed piece of chewed string is sitting in the Cluedo box instead of the lead piping? Not that it stopped Rev Green from using it to bash Mrs Peacock's brains out. Losing the dice was a different matter and not so easy to compensate for. I ALWAYS lost the dice. They should make an app for your phone in case you … oh, they already have.

I often played Battling Tops with my mates but my mum sold our original game for 5p at a car boot sale without even asking me … which is why she didn't realise that we'd changed all the names of the tops with biro so that Smitty was no longer Smarty but Shitty, Tricky Dicky was Pricky – in place of both words if I remember – and Hank ended up doing something which was hardly likely to help his performance in the arena.

I paid £50 recently to get a replacement set but I haven't given it a go yet because it always took SO long to play the blasted thing as a) the string kept breaking and you needed the skills of a seamstress (which were in plentiful supply in the 70s but less so now) to thread it back through and knot it again and b) half the time, the top fell flat on its face as soon as you propelled it through the gate anyway. Or was that just me?

In the old days, we'd quite often play a board game after supper if Mike Yarwood, Dick Emery or the Sweeney weren't on telly. It was meant to calm Dad down after a hard day at work but it usually had the opposite effect, especially if it was Monopoly and he'd been sent straight to jail twice in a row before landing on my property portfolio with its handful of houses and several hotels. He'd insist on playing scrabble with us afterwards and would come up with some unusual words which mum told me not to try looking up in the dictionary.

And at Xmas, after trying to shift portions of pudding from my plate to various hiding places on the dinner table (it helped secure additional helpings with the chance of a foil-wrapped 10p piece inside them) and then watching the seasonal blockbuster on TV (three years after you'd seen it at the cinema and 20 mins shorter because the BBC were even more draconian than those uptight wankers at the BBFC), we'd play Pictionary and pray that we weren't the one to pair up with Dad whose drawings were so meticulous that he'd invariably fail to finish them before the egg timer was up.

My absolute favourite games though were Treasure of the Pharaohs and Haunted House both of which were based on constructing four rooms with two inter-locking L-shaped cards on the board. TOTP (ooh, same initials as Top of the Pops) has made several reappearances over the years (though my original became ant fodder in my obviously not-quite-airtight bottom cupboard) but the family now needs to rely on my recollection of the rules which I tend to make up on the spot and so are a little inconsistent, especially if I've had a beer or two. So, when they ask me what happens when the explorer reaches the bottom of the snake-pit, if it's theirs, it gets to die a slow and painful death, whereas mine is usually allowed to go straight to the treasure chamber and have a shot at winning the game.

I re-purchased Haunted House so that we could play it as a family during lockdown. This was the game where you dropped a ball-bearing down the chimney with its four-way plastic chute which was meant to randomly feed into one of the rooms, giving your counter a 25% chance of being wiped out. In practice, it would always fall the same way meaning you had a 100% chance of snuffing it if you were in the broomstick room and a free pass everywhere else. That said, even then there was a good chance the ball would miss the broomstick altogether which meant, certainly when it was my counter and my rules, that you were immediately declared the winner. I was so excited to play it again but my kids thought it was crap. Sore losers, I say.

I also fished out my old Mastermind game (the ants clearly found the plastic far less appetising than the other cardboard options) for our lockdown championship. This was the code-breaking game with the sinister James Bond villain and his strangely-alluring Asian temptress on the lid, where your opponent had to guess your four-colour code by placing plastic pegs in the correct order and in the least number of attempts. It's called Mastermind but has nothing to do with scary black chairs and Icelandic interrogators (I didn't used to know about their tradition of patrilineal naming so I admit to thinking that Mr & Mrs

Magnusson must have had a particularly warped sense of humour to call their poor son 'Magnus').

It's a game of logic, patience and psychology. I beat everyone this Xmas except my son who paused long enough from rolling his own fags, creating whisky-based cocktails and admiring his tattoos & piercings to guess my cunning combination in just three moves. He then took over Spotify for the rest of the evening and I'm still trying to delete thrash metal songs from my playlist several months later.

It's fair to say that my experiment in weaning my kids off modern electronic games and onto traditional board versions met with mixed success. For one thing, they're a bit clunky (the games not my kids). Any which contain moving parts generally result in you wrecking the whole thing whenever you actually try to move them. Inching up the door to a tomb or spinning a wheel of death invariably sends counters flying and walls crashing down.

They have a lower level of precision too. With electronic games, you have a binary answer to whether you're successful or not – either you move up a level or, like me, you stay on the same one for days on end as you try to work out how to jump over the ditch without burning yourself to death on the flame thrower. Not so with our old games. Regardless of the rules on height clearance, if you could jam the explorer under the Great Stone of Cheops then you were successfully through to the next room, end of. They'd call it a workaround today.

The only non-electronic game my kids now agree to play is Cards Against Humanity. It's their rules which makes it tricky for me to cheat anymore. Monopoly, Cluedo and the others, despite their eclectic mix of non-moving moving parts, dodgy substitutes, missing dice and dog-eared community chest cards, will return to being ant fodder. I'd say they don't know what they're missing but sadly (as this photo proves) they actually do for once.

33 DALLAS

The absolute very first time I began to watch Dallas was the first season it hit our screens back in 1978. Every generation has its favourite drama shows and sitcoms which burn brightly and then disappear (some more quickly and dignified than others – you know who you are, Crossroads) but Dallas clung on with its constant stream of kidnappings, shootings, cancer scares and, er, bad dreams to retain our attention.

The way I'd describe Dallas to my kids is that it's just like Friends if any of the characters were actually friends or even vaguely liked each other. Especially the married ones. To be clear, that's 'just like Friends' not 'Just Good Friends' with Paul Nicholas and Jan Francis (we know he jilted you at the altar, Penny, but he's a lovable rogue so JUST GET BACK TOGETHER).

A lot of Dallas' success in the UK was down to Terry Wogan who would give a round-up of the events at Southfork every week on his Radio 2 show (not that we listened to it in our household – I was too young for Radio 2 and my folks were too old which is one of the many downsides of being conceived by mistake late in life … the other major one being the revelation that you were the consolation prize when your Dad's rugby team got hammered 106-0 in the cup.

Although coining the nickname 'Poison Dwarf' for a young girl would get you thrown off air nowadays, Terry's jibes were generally as good-natured as the digs he made at the Eurovision Song Contest set-up which transformed what would otherwise have been the worst TOTP line-up ever into something approaching cult status. As the great Europhile himself said: "that's the whole point of it, of course, to sneer at foreigners" (which would probably get him sacked today too). Not be outdone, his fellow countryman, Graham Norton, has proved a worthy successor on several occasions, not least when he introduced the German entry as "marmite … if everyone hated marmite".

I remember the opening credits of Dallas pretty well – the aerial shots of one of the least photogenic cities in the world with virtually no landmarks of any note, forcing them to focus on the Dallas Cowboys stadium which meant nothing to anyone in the UK unless they happened to have watched Debbie Does Dallas. Those same purveyors of adult movies would have felt equally at home with the 'wocka chicka' theme tune, courtesy of that sleazy electric guitar and wah wah pedal combination. Classic 70s porn.

I think the whole nation liked to watch how the other half lived – To The Manor Born was a big UK success at the same time – and what shocked us most (in both shows to be honest) was just how incredibly tight-fisted these wealthy sorts were. My mum and dad, like many post-war parents, still thought we were in rationing and so took JR's careful approach with money as a ringing endorsement of their own parsimonious policy. Xmas presents were an orange, chocolate money and a book from the discount shelf at Woolies, fairy liquid was used in the bath because it was cheaper than Matey and hand-me-downs were obligatory no matter that my older brother was twice as big as me at the same age and my sister's sports kit was, strictly speaking, more suitable for netball than rugby. If I complained, my mum told me not to be so ungrateful. She'd be sued nowadays for damaging my mental health.

If any of us kids came back late from a sports match and needed picking up (only if we won – we'd have to walk two miles home otherwise), we were told to ring from the phone box nearest the school and hang up after the pips sounded without putting in any money. This was when phone boxes contained phones rather than books or defibrillators although they also contained prostitutes' calling cards and streams of urine so were best avoided unless, of course, you wanted to ring a brothel or were caught short. Our aborted call was the signal for mum or dad to collect us and it saved 2p every time, meaning that, by the end of our time at school, we'd probably saved enough to buy a strawberry mivvi between the three of us.

Back to the Ewings though. The question about who shot JR gripped the nation, fuelled by a tabloid frenzy on a par with Freddie Starr's unusual eating habits and Harry & Meghan's reluctant waiver of their privacy to make a few constructive comments about the people who'd either funded or attended their lavish wedding. I assumed initially that, being set in Dallas, it was probably Lee Harvey Oswald or the bloke on the grassy knoll but it was actually Kristin … sorry, spoiler alert, it was actually Kristin. He got shot again just over 30 years later when Larry Hagman himself died in real life. Both actor and character had the Dallas theme tune played at their respective funerals. I've told my kids I want 'Big Mouth Strikes Again' played at mine. It's probably my 2nd favourite Smiths track but I reckon it would be a little too odd to have 'Am I Still Ill?' sung when I'm lying there dead. 'Heaven Knows I'm Miserable Now' on the other hand though …

After JR's shooting, the next major controversy was the death of Bobby Ewing. This came as a welcome relief to those of us who'd seen his odd way of swimming in Man from Atlantis and so agreed with Terry

Wogan that he was 'the wettest thing ever to come out of the sea'. It was a joy to see Pam, the lovely Victoria Principal (now a skincare business entrepreneur apparently), liberated from her crushingly-boring relationship. Like Opal Fruits, she was made to make our mouths water and so deserved better. And then what happened? The whole series turned out to be a dream because the American viewing public were clearly far bigger Patrick Duffy fans than us Brits were. In those days, it was quite rare for public opinion to reverse a decision made by the TV bosses. Nowadays it just takes a couple of angry tweets and the whole programme's cancelled.

Those same TV Executives ended up colluding with the competition to create some hype around the Dallas vs Dynasty rivalry to lift ratings – although Oasis & Blur's record companies showed them how to orchestrate it far more effectively a few years later. It didn't really work in our household – we preferred home-grown drama with gritty storylines like Penelope Keith's struggle to win back her family estate and could only take so much US glamour and intrigue – but I gather the introduction of Joan 'Alexis' Collins and her American football-style shoulder pads in series 2 of Die-Nasty was a game-changer.

There were plenty of other US drama shows at the time – Falcon Crest, the Waltons, Bonanza – but none of them got the family together around the TV quite like Dallas. And largely thanks to Terry Wogan, we had a good laugh about it every week too. If only Eurovision was on more often than once a year. Actually, on the other hand, ignore that thought.

There were 357 episodes of Dallas and a further 344 more of the spin-off series, Knots Landing. That's 700 hours of our lives. In contrast, Crossroads ran for 4500 episodes plus the ill-fated extra 320 in 2001-3 which proved such a shitshow that it was brought to a merciful close with the revelation that the whole of the two year revival had been dreamed up by Jane Asher's character. One of Dallas' less-welcome legacies. "Oh fudge" was Jane's final line. Very fitting.

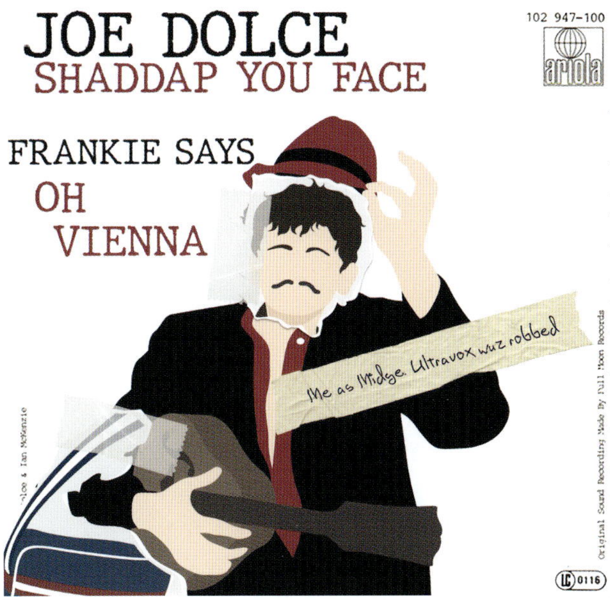

34 ONE HIT WONDERS

The absolute very first time I heard a one-hit wonder was, well you never actually know do you? There were a few acts which you suspected might have limited enduring appeal – for instance, I don't remember wanting to dress up like Fred Wedlock and eagerly wait for his follow-up to the Oldest Swinger in Town – but I certainly thought that Men Without Hats were set for long-term chart success after Safety Dance. I was a teenager wearing a very cool trilby at the time (I was also wearing a denim jacket, cardigan and a Weetabix Neat Wheat Mate T-Shirt – I'll share the photo at the bottom of the story – and therefore couldn't have been more cool) so it would've been far too ironic to write 'Men Without Hats' on my pencil case in tippex … which proved a blessing since, after Safety Dance (in the UK at least), they vanished without a trace and I'd have been forced to pop down to WH Smith and buy a new one.

What I love is the thought that some of these might-have-been pop stars are now accountants or dentists with workmates and clients who presumably have no idea about their 15 minutes of fame. A friend of mine used to work in the same media agency as the guitarist from Department S who, back in the 80s, had asked if Vic was there and in one stroke exhausted their capacity for inventive lyrics before they could pen a follow-up single.

The banjo player in Fiddlers Dram, who liked to remind us about the day we went to Bangor (which rather predictably became 'the day we went to bang 'er' in my boys school), reckons he made £8,000 from the song but had to give half of it to his ex-wife. Apparently, he drank the rest which sounds a little like George Best's line about going broke ("I spent it all on booze, birds and fast cars and the rest I wasted").

John Peel was probably the home of no-hit wonders and no doubt felt deeply ashamed when Joy Division scored their only Top 30 single hit with Love Will Tear Us Apart (this doesn't make them one-hit wonders though – I'm not sure why but it just doesn't). That said, he did propel Althea and Donna to the top of the charts with Uptown Top Ranking before they faded away never to be heard of again ... although I notice that they recently announced some reunion gigs which I assume will be one of the shortest nights out any of us could possibly experience. What on earth do they play for an encore and, if it's Uptown Top Ranking, what on earth did they play beforehand?

Remember Simon Park? I didn't either but he and his orchestra took Eye Level to No.1, keeping the Sweet's Ballroom Blitz off the top. I've just watched the TOTP re-run with the whole orchestra wearing orange polo necks and slacks. It was about as rock 'n' roll as Mr Blobby. It obviously helped that it was the theme tune to Van der Valk, a Dutch detective played by a bloke from Nottingham called Barry and quite a rarity in the days before Danish cop thrillers with sub-titles invaded our TV screens. I'm not sure if this counts as a proper one-hit wonder but I like the song and I've enjoyed watching some early episodes recently to remind myself that the Dutch constabulary in 70s Amsterdam had a strict recruitment policy of non-native speakers, preferably with cockney accents, as did the local criminal fraternity too. They rebooted the series recently with that bloke off Hustle. No, me neither.

There were quite a few others who deserved to be on the OHW list because they were either crap, ridiculously sentimental, silly or all of the above. These include Clive Dunn's Grandad, There's No One Quite

Like Grandma by St Winifred's School Choir and Joe Dolce's Shaddap You Face which, as everyone knows, kept Midge Ure's Ultravox off the top spot and so encouraged him to ditch his Thin Lizzy touring gig (not sure how the pencil moustache, sideburns and new romantic trenchcoat went down with his long-haired and leathered bandmates anyway) and focus fully on the Vox.

A song which didn't fit into the typical OHW categories but whose band name did was Matchstalk Men and Matchstalk Cats & Dogs (I know, the title's pretty silly too but it's about art so let's give it the benefit of the doubt). It was by Brian & Michael which must be the least pop-star name I've ever heard (unless it was ironic – like the Smiths – in which case it's brilliant). What's even better is that the band members were actually called Kevin & Michael so they must have decided, after much deliberation over a pint or two of real ale, that Brian was a more rockstar name than Kevin. Please, please, please let this be true. Brian/Kevin & Michael used fellow OHWs, St Winifreds School Choir, on backing vocals. That might technically disqualify SWSC from the list but it definitely cements B&M on it.

Carl Douglas' Kung Fu Fighting wasn't silly either but it made an army of schoolkids look pretty stupid as we strapped our ties round our heads and aimed karate chops & kung fu kicks at our mates in the playground while grunting 'huh' and 'hah' at regular intervals. Written and performed by a Jamaican (obviously), it was meant to be the B-Side to 'I Want to Give You My Everything' (yawn) but reached No.1 in every country in the western world … except Switzerland where the Swiss were only just going through their Donny & Marie Osmond phase, several months after the rest of Europe, and so chose 'I'm Leaving it All Up to You' (double yawn) ahead of our oriental disco masterpiece.

Another Asian-inspired OHW was Turning Japanese by the Vapors. At my school, the sixth formers would question all the spotty-faced new boys (like me) on the meaning of the song. This was a tricky one to know how to answer safely. If you said it was meant to represent a boy's facial expression during masturbation then you'd be beaten up and greeted with chants of 'wanker' for the next few weeks and, if you pretended not to know the song, you'd be beaten up and have your name scribbled out in biro and replaced with 'saddo' on every school noticeboard. I got round it by admitting I knew the meaning but pointing out it was Eggy who'd told me and so he got beaten up instead.

One of my favourite OHWs was Two Pints of Lager and a Packet of Crisps Please by Splodgenessabounds, which displayed a lyrical inventiveness which Department S could only dream of. It came out in 1980 and was apparently about the trouble Max Splodge had being served in the Crown at Chiselhurst when they called last orders (which is what pubs did in the old days, often accompanied by a bell and usually well before bedtime). I've no idea if this was an apocryphal story (and, if it was, surely he could've lied about something more momentous) but his band consisted of Roger Rodent, Miles Runt Flat, Pat Thetic, Whitty Archer and Baby Greensleeves so you have to doubt their capacity to tell the truth.

It's easy to be dismissive about one-hit wonders but just think how many no-hit wonders exist – either as proper hard-working bands or talentless 'in-our-dreams' would-be pop stars like me? I'd give two pints of lager and any number of packets of crisps for a sniff of their success. I'd sing about any of my elderly relatives if it got me onto TOTP where I'd dance, safely or otherwise and with or without Vic. I'd even go to Bangor, wherever that is, if that's where the BBC had their studio. And, back in the dressing room afterwards, flushed by my longed-for pop fame, I'd be turning Japanese for the rest of the night.

35 MAGIC ROUNDABOUT

The absolute very first time I watched Magic Roundabout might just have been in the late 60s. I would've been under five so suspect I missed all the drug-taking references and simply took the show at face value ie Dougal was a normal paranoid dog with an unusual but entirely innocent desire for 'sugar lumps' and Dylan was one of the few hippies in Britain who wasn't off his tits 90% of the time. And, as for that bouncing pea-headed creature called Zebedee … well, I'd hope that even my toddler self would have had his suspicions.

The show was originally created for French TV (by an English animator called Ivor Wood which sounds like the sort of name we'd dream up at school) but it was Emma Thompson's dad who actually made it funny (the French would hardly have managed that on their own, would they) by coming up with new characters and dialogue based on the original footage. This isn't the first time a bunch of Brits have injected humour into some worthy French nonsense – and I'm thinking Flashing Blade (re-written by Russell T. 'Dr Who' Davies no less), the Battle of Agincourt and the 2012 Olympics when London got the nod over Paris (strictly speaking, those last two aren't actual examples but it's good to remind our Gallic friends of these humiliating defeats every once in a while).

And if you think me poking fun at the French seems a bit too xenophobic, wait until you hear about Emma's dad who steadfastly refused to take his family to a French restaurant, banned berets & striped jumpers from the house and created his 'cheddar and brie' storyline in one of the earlier MR episodes as a deliberate reference to cheese-eating surrender monkeys* so I'm a positive Francophile in comparison.

*ok, I made that last one up ... and the one before (the first one's true though)

The great thing about putting Magic Roundabout on just five minutes before the news was that it encouraged the show's UK team to appeal to both adults and kids, something which happens all the time now (Shrek, Toy Story, every animated film from Disney since 2000) but it was quite the rarity in the 60s & 70s. I've just watched an episode in which Ermintrude (the red-spotted pink cow) comments on nationalising the railways – a classic topic of kindergarten banter – and there's another where, after Zebedee tells everybody that it's time for bed, Florence politely answers "already?" (instead of "who the fuck do you think you are ... my dad?" which is what she should've said) prompting the spring-loaded giant insect with the Sergeant Major moustache to explain it's time for the news ... which of course it really was (thus breaking the 4th wall and paving the way for the Young Ones and Deadpool). Now that's an aside I didn't expect to write when I chose this topic.

Dougal's name outraged the French creators because they thought it was a piss-take of their President, de Gaulle – something which Emma's dad denied in a TV interview but, fingers crossed, he was just messing with their heads even more and it really was a piss-take all along. Dougal looked like a sausage dog (is that what he was? I've never really thought about it – he just didn't have any legs and so would slide around like Brian the snail) and his depressing observations on life came straight from comedian Tony Hancock who, for any younger readers, used to spend a Half Hour entertaining our folks every week on the radio and considerably longer doing the same thing off-air to the wife of Sergeant Wilson off Dad's Army.

Apparently, the cheerfully optimistic Brian was based on Eric Thompson himself whilst Mollie Sugden channelled the essence of Ermintrude to create her Mrs Slocombe character in Are You Being Served (although I don't remember Ermintrude making so many references to her furry friend). By the way, I SO fancied Miss Brahms when I was younger but we didn't have a department store in my home town for me to fantasise about our inevitable meeting and I couldn't really imagine her behind the counter at Woolies weighing up my Pick n Mix (yes, I'm sure there's some sort of innuendo in there somewhere).

Florence, at face value, appeared to be a charming little girl with her rosy cheeks and that cheeky blue bow in her hair but she was also the one who supplied Dougal with his regular fix of 'sugar lumps.' Just saying. And, as for Dylan, he was played by Bill Nighy in the 2004 movie which tells you all you need to know about the character.

As ever, the theme tune was truly memorable (although it sounded like it was recorded on 19th century technology). The opening and closing credits always had Florence and her three young friends (who she ignores for the rest of the programme) bunking off school and riding the horses on the carousel (with one horse mysteriously riderless – why no conspiracy theories on the internet?) while some lecherous old weirdo cranked the music box nearby and leered at them.

Besides the drug references, Magic Roundabout was often hijacked for lazy and cheap comedic purposes (this story being a perfect case in point). In 1975, long before his TV series, his lucrative part-ownership of the rights to 'Who Wants to be a Millionaire' and his daughter turning up on reception in The Office, Jasper Carrott had released a novelty single called Funky Moped which was languishing in the nether regions of the charts. He then happened across one of the two most effective marketing ploys of the 70s/80s to boost sales. Unable to put Plan A into action by convincing ad agency Bartle Bogle Hegarty to feature his song on one of their Levi 501 jeans commercials (not helped by Nick Kamen's striptease in the laundrette still being 10 years away), he did the next best thing and made sure the BBC listened to the B-Side of the single. It was a slightly risqué take on a Magic Roundabout script and, predictably, those pompous old farts at the Beeb promptly banned it, thereby catapulting it into the Top 10 with sales of half a million copies.

Listening to it again, it's pretty tame compared to what came afterwards (a few years later, as I often remind you, Frankie Goes to Hollywood had to tell us all to relax when we wanted to come before they could sit back and wait for Mike Read and his BBC bosses to do the rest) but the suggestion that Florence was not a virgin (apparently 'she drops them for certain') and Dougal's literal response to being told to piss off by Dylan was sufficient provocation for the BBC in the 70s.

Although Eric Thompson's subtle and gentle adult humour was enough to ruffle the feathers of the French creators, Jasper Carrott's sexual innuendo might have been more to their liking (you know how kinky the French are). "Thanks for sticking up for me" says Florence with a wink at Dylan near the end of Jasper's track. "Time for bed" is Dylan's sleazy reply. Touché, mon ami.

36 TV ADVERTS

The absolute very first time I saw some adverts in the 70s & 80s was the moment I realised that my formulaic opener to every story (and this is no.36 so I've had a good run) doesn't work 100% of the time.

What I do remember is the first time I tried to record my favourite ads off the TV because it was so much harder than compiling mix tapes from the Radio One chart show on a Sunday evening. That exercise was tough enough – as I've explained in an earlier story – but at least you sometimes got a heads-up from the DJ about what was coming next. If not, once you'd recognised the opening bars of the tune, you only missed the first 15 seconds meaning you still had a good three minutes or so of your favourite song to enjoy at your leisure later on.

If, on the other hand, you missed recording the first 15 seconds of an advert, you'd only end up with the jingle at the end and would have to wait several days before you got another chance (at which point you were just as likely to make exactly the same mistake again). And it's not as though the Hamlet cigar adverts started with 'Air on the G String' ('dum ... dum ... dum ... dum') to prompt you to press the record button.

I must have sat through three full afternoons of children's telly (I was clearly a popular boy with loads of friends and a full social life) to capture the 30 seconds of magic which I could replay for weeks afterwards. This ought to make me an advertiser's dream except I had no influence on my mum's shopping habits other than forcing her to buy more packets of monkey-marketed PG Tips than she strictly needed – those tea card albums don't fill up themselves you know.

At the time, I made dozens of video tapes which, for some reason, I still keep tucked away in a cupboard despite no longer having a VCR machine to play them. They're mostly recordings off TOTP or The Tube but also include a few adverts which are easy to find because each cassette comes with a folded sheet of paper where I have neatly written out every song, sports clip and advert on the tape. And, no, before you say anything, that's not sad or OCD. That's just sensible.

I think I recorded the ads mostly for the music (but I made an exception in the 90s with Tango – "yes, Ralph, the big orange fella gives him a good old slapping" – which was banned for inciting copycat behaviour in the playground although, when I was younger, we'd have been grateful to get just a slap rather than the usual kicking). Here's some on the list:

- Good Day by Nescafe – so niche I can't even find a YouTube video of it but I remember the song ending with 'this is a welcome change, Beryl' as the two old biddies do a knees-up (or have I made that up?).
- The Baggy Trousers rip-off for Colgate Blue Minty Gel ('mum and dad use it as well'). I also recorded the scene in Grease at Frenchie's house where Jan mimics the Beaver on the 50s toothpaste ad ('brusha, brusha, brusha, get the new Ipana'), the lyrics to which have stirred up heated debate on the internet … and when I say heated, I'm talking "I thought it was brush-up?", "no it's brusha", "oh ok".
- Cadburys Flake – because I liked the chill-out vibe of the song ('only the crumbliest, flakiest chocolate') and nothing to do with the hardcore sexual symbolism with the chocolate blow job and the overflowing bath (I was in my early teens, sexually frustrated and too young to rent out adult movies from Steve the Goth at our local video store – although he did let me have a couple of under-the-counter copies later on and I realised I preferred the Flake ads).

- I also recorded one of the Pepsi ads so I could learn the words to Lipsmackinthirstquenchinacetastinmotivatingoodbuzzincool-talkinhighwalkinfastlivinevergivincoolfizzinPepsi and impress the girls in the Wimpy after school. I was hopeless at it and I blame this failure for me not losing my virginity any earlier than I eventually managed and, no, there won't be a 'Frankie Says …' account of that particular episode of my life, mainly because I need to fill up three sides of A4 for every story and … well, you can guess the rest.

Looking back at these and other 70s/80s adverts, it's striking how different they are to the ones on air today. For a start, there was a stark absence of mixed-race couples on telly in those days but you can't sit through a commercial today without one. I'm not sure how much this reflects a change in British society (I don't get out much anymore) but I guess it's trying to symbolise a more tolerant one. In the old days, if the OXO Dad had come home to find a couple of mixed-race children of his around the supper table, Lynda Bellingham's gravy wouldn't exactly be the first thing he'd be discussing with her.

Another noticeable difference back then was far fewer car commercials and far more ads for coffee and cigars. The Hamlet ones were based on the premise that calamity could be ameliorated by a cheeky puff and a few chords of Bach. That's fine when it's some poor geezer struggling to take passport pictures in a photo booth (that's how your mum & dad used to take selfies, kids) but I've just re-watched one where a peeping Tom runs out of coins to feed the seaside telescope he's using to spy on a girl in a bikini. No wonder advertisers were called Mad Men.

As for coffee, we either had Gareth Hunt with his slightly unsettling coffee bean fist shake and constant stream of new girlfriends or we got the Gold Blend couple with the slow-burn relationship between the woman who ended up marrying Shoestring and the bloke off Buffy the Vampire Slayer. How on earth did that end well?

Here are others which I wasn't sad enough to record on my VCR but secretly wished I had:

- Hai Karate after shave – 'one whiff drives women wild' (and, if you weren't interested in driving women wild you took 'Enry Cooper's advice and slapped on some Brut instead).
- The Milk Tray Man ('All Because the Lady Loves …') which is what your mates called you if you ever went out to a party dressed in black (you've really got to feel for Steve the Goth from the video shop).
- Cadbury Smash Martians – as I've warned you before, Smash came from the home of chocolate but was powdered potato. Someone in Bourneville was clearly having a laugh.
- Reggie Perrin pouring Cinzano over Joan Collins, Campari-drinker Lorraine Chase being wafted here from ~~paradi~~ Luton Airport.
- That dear old boy, JR Hartley, searching for his Fly Fishing book with Yellow Pages (he'd have found it far more quickly with Google).
- 'A second class return to Dottingham' with Tunes plus mum packing off her college son with Vicks Sinex ('course you can, Malcolm').

We were putty in the hands of the advertisers. We flocked to the shops to buy strawberry or blackcurrant Chewitts once we realised they were even chewier than Barrow-in-Furness bus depot (although this wasn't enough to make us eat the banana ones). They made us want just one Cornetto, even if we had to nick it off someone else, and they tried to scare us into drinking milk by warning us of an alarming infestation of something called a 'Humphrey.'

Sadly these days, there's almost certainly something 'problematic' about every single one of these ads which means there's no chance of them being aired today except on social media for the liberal elite to point out how neanderthal we once were. But what those advertisers wouldn't give for a golden era when people actually watched and talked about their adverts in the pub & playground instead of zipping through them on catch-up or skipping them on YouTube. Cue the sound of a lit match in the offices of ad agencies across the land before Air on the G String fills the room.

37 SMASH HITS

The absolute very first time I bought Smash Hits magazine was in the early 80s because I wanted to know the words to Stand & Deliver and find out what Adam actually sang since it sounded an awful lot like 'da diddly qua qua' or some equally unlikely nonsense. I found out later from 'ver Hits' that it was indeed 'da diddley qua qua' after all which meant my 30p was completely wasted. I could buy a hi-fi with that nowadays if they still made them.

Smash Hits began in the late 70s and was the main source of posters on any schoolkid's wall. It was also the only source of lyrics unless your favourite band/artist happened to print them on the inside of the record sleeve (the Smiths were particularly helpful in this regard). Adam did the same thing too but the album came out months after the single and I didn't want to wait that long singing the wrong lyrics if the actual words were 'Bo Diddley, cry cry' instead. I finally got the Prince Charming album as a Xmas present which is just as well because Ant Rap was released earlier that month so I only had a couple of weeks singing 'Marco, Merrick, Dairylea' before I could correct myself. I did think it was odd he'd sing about cheese triangles but it wasn't long after he'd suggested we should 'leapfrog the dog and brush me daddy-o' so, frankly, anything was possible.

Misheard lyrics (called mondegreens apparently, who knew?!) were such a common problem in our day that Maxell came up with a couple of adverts taking the mickey out of them with blokes holding cards of nonsense lines which sounded uncannily like the songs themselves. Desmond Dekker's Israelites became 'me ears are alight' ('darling cheeseheads I was yards too greasy') and the Skids sang 'into the valley, peas sure sound divine' instead of … well, perhaps those were the actual lyrics – I didn't get that particular issue of Smash Hits to check.

The magazine was published by Emap whose head office was based near my home town. The dad of a friend of mine from primary school used to work there but Smash Hits didn't come out until I'd moved to secondary school and I'd fallen out with him by then (the boy that is – I remained on good terms with his dad). I offered him a walnut whip to try and get back in his good books but he said he didn't like the nut on the top. Er, so what? 99% of us didn't like the nut on top but it didn't stop us enjoying the rest of it.

When I was reading the magazine (OK, checking out the lyrics and tearing out pictures of Siouxsie & the Banshees to blu-tack onto my wall), it was selling half a million copies every issue which is as much as that magazine monster Radio Times shifts today (and, at an equally-monstrous £3.50, it's probably the only thing keeping WH Smiths from going bust). With those readership figures, just like TOTP's audiences of 19 million during the same period, no one could ignore Smash Hits if they wanted to sell some records. Paul Weller described the magazine 'as though punk rock had never happened' but that didn't seem to stop him from coming back for interviews to nudge 'Town Called Malice' or one of his Style Council numbers into the Top 10.

This was long before cooler magazines like Q, Mojo and, by a couple of years, The Face had hit the newsstands (that's what they did in the old days – sometimes your newsagent would deliver them but, if it was WH Smiths, you were just as likely to get Woman's Realm or National Geographic land on your doormat instead of what you'd actually ordered). And if NME and Melody Maker were too grown-up for you, Smash Hits was your early-teens alternative once you'd moved on from Look-In. There were some interesting writers – Neil Tennant was on the staff in the early days, fresh from the editor role at the UK offices of Marvel Comics, before he headed off to Pet Shop Boys stardom (two jobs which are even better than being a pop star surely?).

The writers and editors were surprisingly irreverent (or possibly just childish). They called Morten from A-Ha 'Snorten, Forten, Horten' because that's how they thought Norwegians spoke (as opposed to Swedes who, as all Muppets fans knew, made hurdy gurdy noises instead). Paul McCartney was 'Fab Macca Wacky Thumbs Aloft' (well, I guess that is what he did a lot of the time so it was fair enough) and Smiley Minogue presumably got her nickname for similar reasons (though let's hope this didn't apply when she heartlessly dumped Jason over the phone from Michael Hutchence's hotel room in Japan). And every time they mentioned Duran Duran, they referred to 'pop' 'star' Simon Le Bon which might be harsh (I saw him play Isle of Wight Festival not so long ago) but, in hindsight, was pretty funny.

In their interviews, they would ask their pop celeb fodder silly questions like whether they preferred cats or if their mums played golf or what colour was January and they made up their own language – bands boozed on 'rock n roll mouthwash,' female singers were 'foxtresses' and 'pur-lease' was the response if (by which I mean when) the interviewees said something ludicrous. I've just looked back at some old covers and one of them trumpeted an exposé about why Kylie was scared of

Bob The Builder. The editorial style wasn't a complete piss-take like Viz though. They came over as fans just like the rest of us but they basically pricked the pomposity and mythology around stardom whilst remaining part of the carnival.

Something that I found confusing at the time but great in hindsight was how they'd include pieces on the Smiths or Echo and the Bunnymen in the same issue as they interviewed Five Star or Rod Stewart. If you were looking to graduate onto the NME or Melody Maker, with an emerging sense of self-importance as a follower of 'serious' music, it was tough to buy a magazine with Kajagoogoo on the cover just because you wanted to read an article about the Goo Goo Dolls inside (they may not quite have overlapped but I couldn't resist the wordplay).

Nowadays, PR people with copy approval would run a red pen through most of the articles penned by the early Smash Hits contributors, ensuring that the end result was as bland, uninformative and inoffensive as anything remotely similar on sale today. I loved how the writers refused to pander to the celebs (without completely alienating them either) in the way ALL media – social or mainstream – does today, especially if it involves their mental health, charidee work or fatuous virtue-signalling 'beliefs'. In fact, doing a bit of research on the magazine has vastly increased my appreciation of the publication. Pricking pomposity with a bit of humour and irreverence, but with an appropriate level of respect too, is exactly what we need right now.

Alternatively, we could just settle for today's status quo (no, not Francis, Rick & co) where journalists & interviewers simply offer a platform for 'pop' 'stars' to lecture us on white privilege, mis-pronouning or causing the destruction of the planet. Next, as Constable Savage on Not the Nine O'Clock News once warned us, we'll be hauled over the coals for walking on the cracks in the pavement or loitering with intent to use a pedestrian crossing or coughing without due care and attention (oh hold on, that probably is a criminal offence now isn't it?). Is that what we want and what our kids deserve? Pur-lease.

38 CHRONICLES OF NARNIA

The absolute very first time I began to read the Chronicles of Narnia, kicking off with The Lion, the Witch and the Wardrobe, was several years after I'd battled through the Peter & Jane Ladybird Book adventures (and I use that final word loosely) and once I'd put Olga da Polga and Paddington behind me. After guinea pigs who told tall stories and talking bears from darkest Peru, I was clearly ready for a messianic lion and an inter-dimensional portal at the back of someone's closet.

It was also the absolute very first time I got a, you know, 'tingling' when I read about Edmund getting hypnotised by the white witch. To be honest, that was my sexual awakening, a time when the veil of naiveté dropped momentarily from my eyes and I snatched a brief glimpse of the man I was destined to become. I was 38 at the time and a late developer.

The titles of the books were magical and I have genuinely felt a thrill (no, not that sort this time) to run through them all again. Besides the opener, the set included Prince Caspian, the Silver Chair and the Voyage of the Dawn Treader (how can a story not be good with the word 'voyage' in the title? And the answer to that is if it's called 'Voyage to the Planet of the Prehistoric Women' which was made into a film by an Oscar nominee who married Bruce Willis' partner in Moonlighting).

Although they were written in the early 50s, I don't remember them seeming dated or old-fashioned when we read them originally. Sadly, I don't think that means they weren't dated and old-fashioned ... it just means we were too.

There's been some scholarly debate about the actual order in which the books are meant to be read (what else have our greatest brains got to do? Oh yes, find a permanent cure for COVID or save the planet would help for starters). When I was younger, I'm sure I went the traditional route (ie the order they were written & published in) and so left the prequel – the Magician's Nephew – until later on. Despite the name of the Last Battle being a bit of a giveaway, I managed to leave the Horse and His Boy until the end for some reason though. I suspect it was on loan from my local library when I tried to read it in the correct order (and that's probably the last time I ever visited a public library which may well mean that at least one of the books in my own Narnia collection is more than a little overdue).

CS Lewis – he was Clive Staples Lewis which sounds like a description of the goings-on in my primary school classroom – was a Professor of English at Oxford University whilst JRR 'Lord of the Rings' Tolkien was in the same faculty. They were mates and members of the Inklings which sounds like a cool band but almost certainly wasn't. How incredible is that? It just needed their equally-initialled (is that a requirement in the job description?) fantasy writer, JK Rowling, to come along a little earlier and join them in the Inklings for us to get the full set. That said, she wouldn't have been allowed into a boys club back then because she was a biological female which, ironically, is the exact opposite of what she tends to get a ton of grief about nowadays. It's a weird world isn't it.

The books are banned in US schools on account of their 'graphic violence, mysticism and gore' (which is more than a little ironic coming from our transatlantic friends) as well as a religious undercurrent which is 'likely to be offensive to non-Christians'. With that logic, the Tale of Mrs Tiggy-Winkle ought to be banned because it's likely to offend non-hedgehogs. In fact, they ought to ban 95% of books since the social media vigilantes are bound to dig up someone who could find the content triggering. What was that? Oh, they already have.

There's clearly plenty of Christian symbolism in the books – Clive was the son of a clergyman's daughter from Ireland after all – but, even in the old days, there were mutterings about religious propaganda aimed at indoctrinating impressionable young minds. That didn't bother us in the slightest when we were reading them but then we never had the culture police to protect us at the time (other than that busybody, Mary Whitehouse, and even she'd seem positively progressive compared to the witchfinders today).

Edmund betrays his family, not for 30 pieces of silver but for a few Turkish delight, but then so did half of Shakespeare's characters too (Brutus, Iago, Macbeth) although, admittedly, not usually for a bag of sugar confectionery. Slightly more pointedly, Aslan (that's the lion) allows himself to be sacrificed to save his people, only to rise again a little while later which, even to an atheist like me (yes, I read the Narnia books and yet somehow slipped through the net), seems a pretty clear reference to JC (and, no, I don't mean the Comic Messiah, John Cleese). That didn't seem to stop old Clive from dismissing these theories as "pure moonshine" which presumably encouraged his fellow intellectuals in the Inklings, at their weekly society meeting, to rub their jaws vigorously and mutter "Jimmy Hill" and "chinny reck-on" during the scholarly debate.

Regardless of the religious overtones, the epic tales of good vs evil made the books perfect candidates for screen adaptation. Spurred on by the success of Peter Jackson and his Lord of the Rings films, along with the impressive box office figures for Harry Potter, Disney were handed the licence to print money with the Narnia franchise in 2005. Ker-ching surely? All they had to do was follow the tried and tested formula of annual releases filmed in New Zealand with a cast of British acting royalty and unknown kids who would no doubt be catapulted to stardom before proving their loyalty to be a few notches lower than their bank balances by laying into their benefactor as a belated thank you (you know who are you are, Daniel, Emma & Rupert).

The franchise got off to a good start with Tilda Swinton, Liam Neeson & James McAvoy (tick) and their NZ locations (tick) propelling The Lion, the Witch and the Wardrobe to become the 4th highest grossing film of that year (double tick). It all went a bit Pete Tong after that though, when they forgot the golden rules of sequels – bring them out once a year (the next two Narnia films trickled out three and five years later) and make them as good if not better than the first one. Watch Prince Caspian to check how far they fell short on this measure too – in fact, save yourself the torture and just take my word for it.

Hopefully, though, someone (Netflix probably) will harness the passion, vision and clout required to bring these stories to life on the screen and introduce Narnia to a new generation. Like our own generation many years before, it will encourage them to explore the back of their parents' wardrobe in the hope of discovering something magical. Sadly, they're likely to get an unpleasant surprise when they end up discovering what sort of stuff their parents regard as magical enough to hide at the back of the wardrobe in the mistaken belief that it's the last place their kids will ever look.

And, if Netflix passes on Narnia, they ought to pick up the rights to the Peter & Jane Ladybird books instead. They might not have talking lions and magical journeys but they're full of misbehaving cats and trips to the greengrocers. And, as far as I remember at least, they pose little to no risk of religious radicalisation. Or did I just miss that again?

Here's my set. Before anyone complains, I'm not suggesting any particular reading order – it's just the way they came off my bookshelf.

39 VIDEO CASSETTES

The absolute very first time I taped something off the telly onto a video cassette was Ghost Town by the Specials because we'd bought the VCR to record my Dad on Look East and I was practicing beforehand with Terry Hall and his band to make sure I got the hang of it. He was being interviewed before a big rugby game (Dad not Terry) because our local club had got through to the 2nd Round of the John Player Cup in the days when most sporting competitions were sponsored by fag brands. Dad made a joke in the interview and was very proud of himself. I was secretly proud of him too but I clearly never let him know.

There was definitely something cool and space-age about video cassettes when they first came out. The way you loaded them into the slot and just pressed them gently forward to make them disappear into the machine with that satisfying whirr and clunk. I know we've got our entire record collection on something we hold in our hand nowadays but, in the 80s, this was cutting edge hi-tech and made you feel like you were one step away from wielding a sonic screwdriver or joining Blake's Seven.

I mentioned in an earlier blog that I'd still got a number of video cassettes in my cupboard and, although I have nothing to play them on, I know exactly what's on them because I have the contents lists I prepared at the time. Not only does this show that being OCD (ie a bloke) has its advantages sometimes but it also proves that I suffered from a mental health condition long before it became trendy to announce it to the world and his wife.

They are mix tapes of songs, adverts and entire series of Not The Nine O'Clock News and the Young Ones. Sadly, I was too late to record Michael Bentine's Potty Time – there are a few episodes on YouTube which I'd recommend you watch but only when your kids are out of earshot otherwise the next knock on the door you hear will be the police.

They bring back bitter-sweet memories of the challenges we faced:

1. The first VCRs were bloody difficult to programme and deliberately designed to catch you out at every step. This was particularly embarrassing if, as the youngest and therefore the most technologically-savvy member of the family, you were entrusted with taping the Xmas blockbuster or, even worse, the Queen's Speech for everyone to settle round the telly to watch later. Successfully recording your father on his TV debut gave you a few credits in the bank but it's amazing how quickly you can use those up by cutting off Her Majesty before she gets to talk about her annus, no matter how horribilis it had been.

2. You set the VCR for a specific date & time, not a specific programme, and so if the BBC were running late (something they were extremely reliable at doing in the 70s & 80s), you ended up taping most of Tomorrow's World and just the opening credits of TOTP. That would give you lots of Raymond Baxter and his parker pen but not much Simon Bates and his hairy cornflake … although you'd get Johnny Dankworth's TW theme tune in either case – bap, bap, bap, bap, BAH, d-duh, duh, duh, duh, duh-nuh. You know the rest.

3. Cassettes were expensive so we were encouraged to re-use them. This was fine if you taped over stuff you'd already watched – Happy Days ("heyyyyy") or Diff'rent Strokes ("what you talking about, Willis") – but, if it was the last episode of Jewel in the Crown or Brideshead Revisited which got wiped, mum had to wait two years for it to be repeated on TV before she could finish the series. That's a long time to be confined to the doghouse.

Most of my pre-recorded videos went to a car boot sale (a sort of DIY eBay) several years ago once I'd realised I could watch them all on YouTube for free. I still had a few left over and they've proved very useful in propping up the heavier shelves in my garage. And, if they ever make a comeback like vinyl (they won't), I'm sure I could replace them with other obsolete stuff of shelf-supporting potential lying around the house which even eBay wouldn't be able to find a home for – I'm thinking atlases & maps, CDs/DVDs, reference books, Yellow Pages, chequebooks and my debut novel just to name a few.

Nowadays, I try and catch all the 80s music documentaries on TV. If I manage to persuade my kids to watch them with me (and, when I say 'watch', I clearly mean 'glance up from their iPhones every once in a while'), they are always amazed (and no doubt secretly proud but the little devils take after their dad and don't let on) how I can point out what people in the crowd are just about to do or what the presenters are going to say on every TOTP clip shown. They think they're the first generation to re-watch memes continually but me & my mates would throw all-nighters replaying those clips to dissect every aspect of them.

That's how we were able to dance like Roland (the less attractive but more talented half of Tears for Fears) in the Mad World video because we studied every move he made – a routine we'd put into practice on the dancefloor at the school disco to huge acclaim. I didn't need to be told it was the highlight of the evening because, out of the corner of my eye, I could see people in the crowd doubled over with laughter and beckoning their mates over to copy the shapes we were throwing.

It's a shame that iPhones didn't exist back then because I'm bound to have gone viral and, 40 years later, I'd be watching my dance masterclass on YouTube with my kids to make them even MORE proud of me (if that were possible). That said, I also copied dance moves off 'Walk Like An Egyptian' by the Bangles and the Madness 'Nightboat to Cairo' track, either of which would get me arrested if they were shown today.

Luckily I didn't try to replicate all my music videos. I remember loving the ones for Safety Dance & Down Under but I'm not sure I could've ever captured the irony of their moves (er, they were ironic weren't they?). And thank god I never recorded Agadoo and learnt the routine. What on earth were we all thinking?

I did record the Smiths' first TOTP appearances though and headed to the next school disco with the glasses & hearing aid I 'borrowed' from my grandad and my mum's favourite flowers jammed down my jeans (they were freesias not gladioli but I wasn't a horticultural expert in my teens) before chickening out at the last minute. My schoolmates were hugely disappointed – they'd only turned up to watch me dance – so I did a cheeky moonwalk for them and that cheered them up no end.

It's funny how the things that superseded video cassettes – DVDs – and audio tapes & vinyl – CDs – have themselves been made redundant by streaming and downloads. It's hard not to see this as progress but it means you can no longer make mix tapes of videos like you used to in the old days (or perhaps you can but I haven't worked out how). Just like the ritual of placing a vinyl on the turntable and attempting to drop the needle on the track you were searching for without scratching the record, there was also something empowering about gently pushing the video cassette into the VCR, pressing record and sitting back with a false sense of security as Peter Powell's intro on TOTP inadvertently taped over the only TV appearance your Dad would ever make.

And, assuming I'm unable to play my video cassettes again, I'll need to recreate the lost memories by getting my wife to video me after I've had a few beers at the next Rewind 80s Festival and recaptured my inner-Roland. Now that's a Tik Tok sensation just waiting to be discovered.

40 NEW ROMANTICS

The absolute very first time I saw a new romantic was the first party I went to after Visage had been on TOTP with Fade to Grey and my mate Stumpy turned up in full make-up, a frilly shirt, baggy trousers and more scarves than M&S. Just a few days before, he'd been wearing bondage trousers and a T-Shirt which advised us to have a holiday in Cambodia (it sounded very exotic) so this was quite a transformation.

His spiky hair had gone too, to be replaced by a long fringe (and when I say long I mean down to his chin) which completely covered half of his face and one of his eyes. Later in life, he claimed that the experience permanently damaged his sight but, boy, he got a lot of attention that night so it was clearly a sacrifice worth making. Phil Oakey of the Human League sported the same look a year later but he was a little older than us and lived 100 miles away in Sheffield so it's unlikely, but not inconceivable, he stole it from Stumpy.

Within weeks, every music-loving member of the boys or girls schools in my home town had ripped posters of Duran Duran & Spandau Ballet out of Smash Hits and blu-tacked them over the top of The Clash & Siouxsie Sioux on their bedroom wall. Pixie boots & winklepickers began deforming adolescent feet and Middle Eastern scarves made our middle England home town look like an outpost of the Gaza Strip.

In the early 80s, cultural appropriation was yet to be made a criminal offence but that didn't stop one of the boys in our school, as he marched down the High St like Yasser Arafat, being accosted by a very large Jewish lady who rightly suspected that he had no idea what he was wearing and why. He defended himself saying it was 'just the fashion' although he had his scarf over his school uniform at the time which rather undermined his argument.

Talking of shameless peacocks, I bumped into Gary Kemp, the song-writing talent behind Spandau Ballet, at a private work party in the early 90s in a London club. I don't think he was in the Finance or HR department but he'd blagged his way in and was propping up the bar on his own (I'm not sure if he'd had his bust-up with lead singer Tony Hadley by then but he certainly looked like Norman No-Friends). I plucked up the courage to ask him what the lyrics to The Freeze were because they sounded a lot like 'blue sing la lune, sing lagoon' which seemed as likely as Adam Ant singing 'da diddley qua qua'. He was quite dismissive, saying he had no idea before turning his back on me, so I told him it was my fault for asking the keyboardist and I should try to track down Tony Hadley because he was obviously the one who wrote all the songs. I may have had a couple of drinks by then.

New Romanticism was seen as a counter-movement to punk's aggressive masculinity and anti-fashion philosophy. Spandau Ballet sang that they were beautiful and clean and so very, very young – all three of which are now just a distant memory to me, if they ever applied at all. The epicentre was London's Blitz club, run by Steve Strange and Rusty Egan (who went on to form Visage with Midge Ure). Boy George was in charge of the cloakroom which was like putting a kid in charge of the sweet shop because he dipped his fingers into every wallet and handbag he was asked to look after. Steve Strange had a strict door policy which almost certainly would have excluded me from getting in, even if I'd managed to make the long journey down to London ("what do you mean you don't like my tank top, Steve, it's from the East

Anglian branch of Fosters Menswear I'll have you know"). He famously barred Mick Jagger from entry so I would've been in good company.

In my defence and in the absence of social media (the only things digital in those days were our watches), any new musical or fashion movement took months to catch on ... and, if you're were in my home town in the sticks, it took twice as long as that. The Blitz Club regulars probably hated that uncool kids in uncool towns like mine would dress up like them several months after they'd moved on to their new look. It may have seemed SO passé to them but, to us, it was an exciting adventure which we all got to share together in our local community and feel like we were part of something bigger. Let us have that moment surely?

By 1984, New Romanticism was finally brought to a close by Band Aid which proved to all of us, no matter where we lived in the UK, that these fresh, edgy bands were mainstream now and even our parents would sing along to them (one of their biggest fans even married into royalty to make sure she got a good seat at Live Aid the following year). It was a signal for the nation's youth to move onto something new ... and that ended up being Stock Aitken & Waterman and the same formulaic sound for the next five years so be careful what you wish for.

I've only put on two parties of my own since I left college – one soon afterwards and the other to mark my 50th birthday some 25 years later – and both of them had the theme of 'come as your favourite musical era' (if it works, and it obviously did from a straw poll of the five people who turned up to the first one, why change it?). This was an undisguised excuse for me to dig out my old winklepickers & scarves and combine them with my Dad's army beret and my first suit trousers which, fortunately for me, were fashionably baggy in the 80s and so not only fitted me but looked the part too. Second time round though, the legs finished halfway up my calves and made me look like MC 'You can't touch this' Hammer. I assume they'd either shrunk or I'd had an unlikely growth spurt in my 30s & 40s. The only other possibility is that my arse had doubled in size in the intervening years which is so far-fetched that I refuse to consider it as an option.

For the second party, I did without the Adam Ant white stripe across the bridge of my nose because I'd been reminded (by Adam) that 'Ant Music was for Sex People' and, having turned 50, I'd clearly left that community behind many years earlier. Originally, I'd played the Durannies, Spandau, Visage, Human League, Thompson Twins, Soft Cell, Ultravox & Blancmange. 25 years later, I'd moved on to … well, it was basically the same playlist but on an iPhone rather than a mix tape recorded off the radio which meant I could dispense with the Peter Powell and Dave Lee Travis intros.

I met Tony Hadley after the more recent party (not straight afterwards that is – he didn't actually get invited or, if he did, he certainly didn't bother showing up). We had both chosen to go on holiday to Rhodes at the same time, although we'd made our way there separately. My wife and I were sitting near him on the beach and I was on the verge of asking him my standard Spandau chat-up line about the lyrics of The Freeze when I overheard him telling his wife how sad he was that he'd fallen out with Gary and that Spandau Ballet had split up, apparently putting the blame for this bust-up on some drunken fan who'd accosted Gary when he was minding his own business at a private function he'd been asked to attend and wound him up about his role in the band.

Forget about Band Aid, I lay the death of the New Romantic movement squarely at the door of that thoughtless, inebriated idiot who managed to cut what could have been a long story short and deprive us of future gold. I know this much is true so why do I find it hard to write the next line?

Isn't it great to see all these bands on the retro festival circuit? Well, "no" is often the answer and even the good ones are neither new nor particularly romantic anymore. This is me, in the late 80s, at my 1st 'favourite musical era' party. I chose 'the early 80s' to show off my deep historical knowledge of popular music. I also drank two cans of beer. At the same time.

41 PLAY SCHOOL

The absolute very first time I watched Play School was, appropriately, when I was very young. I'd just finished working out which flowerpot man was to blame for various horticultural calamities ("was it Bill or was it Ben?") and suddenly I was thrown into the world of weird-shaped windows and that dysfunctional family of soft toys.

We all remember the opener: "Here's a house, here's a door, windows 1 2 3 4. Ready to play, what's the day?" There was a pause before telling us the answer so that we could shout out ourselves ... unless we had an older brother who would butt in and deliberately chirp up with the wrong day. At least I think it was deliberate.

All the presenters were legends – Derek Griffiths, Floella Benjamin, Johnny Ball (Zoe's dad), Toni Arthur et al – but Brian Cant was the man. He was our Mr Play School. He was the Frank Bough of children's TV for us. Frank used to live down the road from me but, as far as I know, Brian didn't. Cant (my predictive text keeps wanting to change his name to can't … but we all know that he absolutely could and did) beat Oliver Postgate to the title of Best-Loved voice on children's TV. Oliver gave us Bagpuss & Ivor the Engine and so represented a formidable challenge but Brian had Trumpton, Camberwick Green & Chigley as well as Play School on his CV so came up trumps.

Apparently, Rick Jones – the slightly scary-looking bloke who stuck his finger up a mouse to create Fingerbobs and looked like the Master off Dr Who – used to smoke dope on the Play School set. Even cuddly Johnny Ball (prior to his Think of a Number gig) was prone to the odd on-air expletive when Ka-too, the imaginatively named cockatoo, bit him during a live segment. If it was a number he was thinking of, I'm pretty sure it must have been 'four' … or at least that's what it sounded like.

We weren't allowed a story until we had managed to tell Brian & co what time it was on the giant clock and – they certainly made us work for it in those days – we were also forced to guess which window we were going to have the dubious pleasure of looking through. It was either the round, square or arched one (apparently there was a triangular one later which must have been confusing for any toddler in the 80s whose bedroom didn't happen to be in the attic) but it didn't really matter which was chosen because we always ended up seeing something boring being made in a factory, the signal for many of us to spend the following few minutes playing with our fuzzy felt or drawing flowers with our spirograph instead.

Besides the presenters, the real stars of the show were the soft toys. The legendary line-up went like this:

i. Big Ted & Little Ted – OK, no problem. Just standard teddy bears. Big one, small one. Nothing to see here – move on.

ii. Jemima – she had dreadlocks and pink/white striped leggings but her dresses looked like they'd been made out of whatever duster was left lying around the set after the cleaners had gone.

iii. Humpty – a green Scottish egg. Now, this was starting to get a bit weird.

iv. Hamble – oh my sweet Jesus. This thing was evil. Apparently, Brian Cant used to kick her around the studio and Rick 'Fingerbobs' Jones used to … well, let's not go there.

It's telling that, when you look at the overseas versions of the show, they stick pretty closely to the roster of toys used in the UK … with one notable exception every time. We may have been the world leader in children's TV – the gold standard which every nation looked up to – but it's fair to say that no other country took a gamble with Hamble.

There were so many dungarees sported by the various presenters that, at times, it looked like they were filming from Greenham Common. Many of them also moonlighted on the spin-off, Play Away, which I'd watch from time to time despite it being too grown-up for me. I mean it had Jeremy Irons presenting it for goodness sake! Even the theme tune sounded like a hit single which wouldn't have seemed out of place on TOTP – in fact, compared to the Goodies' Funky Gibbon and Chuck Berry's My Ding-A-Ling, it was positively the height of sophistication (google it and remind yourself how catchy it was).

Play School was the forerunner of Teletubbies, whose variously-shaped windows were housed somewhere between their heads and their chubby little furry legs. Mr Fingerbobs would've thought he was on a seriously-bad trip. Or perhaps a good one? The show itself was cancelled in 1988, soon after they ditched the windows and decided to refer to 'shapes' instead in some trendy revamp which resulted in everyone losing interest. Take note, Dr Who producers.

There were 5500 editions broadcast but the Beeb decided to wipe two thirds of those so it could preserve Kate O'Mara's ferry shenanigans on Triangle for posterity instead. At its height in the early 80s, the show attracted 5m viewers daily which was half as many as Dr Who at the time and twice as many as it musters today. Just saying.

As for the presenters, Toni Arthur is now a Buddhist and Rick Jones sadly smoked his final spliff not long ago. Johnny Ball is still Zoe's Dad but, at 80+, finds it a little more difficult to think of a number nowadays. His stint on Strictly Come Dancing turned sour when he accused his dancing partner of feigning a broken leg just to avoid tangoing with him. At least she didn't bite him.

Of them all, Floella Benjamin has arguably proved the most successful in post-Play School life. She's a Dame, a Lib Dem and has a statue erected outside the University of Exeter to celebrate her courage (presumably for openly admitting to being a Lib Dem). And, as for Brian, having received neither a gong from the Queen nor a statue from an educational establishment, he left us several years ago to look through those arched windows in the sky. Gone but never forgotten.

Goodbye, until it's our turn to be here again.

Someone wrote on my Facebook page that they'd gone to school with Brian Cant's kids. How fantastic must that have been to have Brian as your Dad? Unless he was fed up reading stories to kids by the time you went to bed, that is.

42 LIVE AID

The absolute very first time I saw Live Aid was, well, live on July 13th 1985. I'd finished school the year before and had just returned from a 'gap yah' round Asia where I'd contracted dysentery and dengue fever before limping home, exhausted and half-starved, to be met with an event which, to all extents and purposes, looked like it was being staged specifically on my behalf. I never saw a bloody penny though. That Irish bloke must have kept the lot.

As most people know, Michael Buerk's feature on the Ethiopian famine inspired Bob Geldof & Midge Ure to launch Band Aid but the idea for Live Aid seems to have come from Boy George after Culture Club played Wembley Arena and some of their Band Aid chums joined them on stage for an encore rendition of Do They Know It's Christmas.

It's difficult for kids today to understand just how unusual and ground-breaking Live Aid was in 1985. For a start, it lasted 16 hours from midday in London to the close in Philadelphia. And it was shown live on the BBC – yes, real 'live' not TOTP miming 'live.' You didn't get Glasto live-streamed in those days so this was at least 15 hours more than the Beeb had ever devoted to music in one go before. Up until then, their gig output consisted solely of the Old Grey Whistle Test which, as you know, the stuffed shirts at the BBC did their utmost to deter young people from watching by hiding it late at night on BBC2 (in our day, 10pm was late at night and no one under the age of 25 watched BBC2 except for half an hour at 9pm) and choosing a name which their research confirmed was the least likely to reflect the content of the show.

The hype about the event had even reached my quiet middle England market town but, in those pre-social media days, it was hard to find out the line-up unless the Radio Times happened to print it which would've been far too helpful and so highly unlikely. I was praying the Smiths might get a shot (although I suppose 'Big Mouth Strikes Again' might not have gone down well at a fundraiser for famine support) but Bob chose legendary chart-toppers Howard Jones and Nik Kershaw instead.

The weather was surprisingly good for a July in the UK, leading one newspaper to comment that even God was on Bob's side although, if that was the case and given his omnipotence, we might have hoped for a better divine contribution to famine relief than decent weather at the benefit concert.

Here are the highlights:

- Status Quo opened the Wembley event at midday with Rockin All Over The World - you've got to love Francis, Rick and the boys haven't you?
- Multi-million sellers Adam Ant & Elvis Costello only got to do just one song each while Nik Kershaw was offered four (yes, FOUR) which was basically his entire singles output. Ultravox were also allowed four and even the Boomtown Rats got to do three – hmmm, I wonder how those two bands managed to sneak onto the line-up?
- Howard Jones only got to do a single song too but, for some reason, chose the one with the poorest chart position in the UK and which the Americans hated so much it didn't even make the Billboard 100.
- Adam, slightly misreading the publicity opportunity of playing to 1.9 billion people, decided that his one song would be a future single which no one knew and was crap anyway. You had ten Top 10 hits to choose from, mate, were you nuts? What was that? Oh, right, sorry to hear it.
- Bryan Ferry, forgetting he'd been a member of Roxy Music with unfettered access to their full back catalogue of chart-toppers, decided instead to perform two unknown tracks off his latest album and ignore the obvious merits of 'Let's Stick Together' at an event to unite the global community.
- In contrast, Queen took the whole thing deadly seriously and hired out a small theatre in Kings Cross for a week to nail their set. They squeezed six songs into the same timeslot in which others sang four and were rightly acclaimed as the best performers on the day.
- Elton John & David Bowie only turned up because Bob told each of them that the other had already agreed to play. Elton spat out his dummy after the Queen set, accusing 'those bastards of stealing the show' which he subsequently insisted was just a light-hearted joke.

That's the Elton John of an alternative universe who's more famous for his banter than his tantrums and hissy fits.

- Phil Collins jumped onto Concorde and flew to the US so he could play both stages, no doubt sticking his hand in the fund-raising pot so the Ethiopians could cover the costs of the flight.
- U2 only did two numbers because Bono decided to dance with a member of the audience instead of squeezing in a third song – this palaver took ten minutes, nine of which were actually spent picking the girl and hauling her out of the crowd rather than actually dancing.
- The Who had technical issues, losing the sound, ironically, just as Rog was singing 'why don't you all f-f-fade away.' And Macca had his usual glitch too (remember the sound loss at the London Olympics?). You could almost hear John Lennon sniggering up there on the right hand of his slightly less popular mate.

The acts were punctuated (I mean unnecessarily-interrupted) by contributions from Germany, Holland, Yugoslavia, Russia, Norway and Japan to make the event appear global rather than merely transatlantic. In those days, these were the slots which signalled a tea or loo break but nowadays they'd be the headline acts.

The US line-up was absolute pop royalty but their section didn't go quite as smoothly as ours (come on, be honest, we were secretly pleased weren't we?). It was the same with the Band Aid vs We Are The World singles – OK, they raised a bit more cash than us but our song was far better than their effort and that was all that really mattered surely?

- They had Madonna, Beach Boys, a chronically under-rehearsed Led Zeppelin, Mick Jagger & Tina Turner (plenty of sex but no sexual chemistry – like watching your parents grope each other in public while slightly tipsy), Bob Dylan (who took the opportunity to criticise the event – nice touch) and, er, the Thompson Twins who, much as I have a soft spot for them, proved they weren't exactly a stadium band.

- The moving video of the famine, set to the Cars' Drive soundtrack, had the biggest impact on UK donations but the US networks didn't show it because they decided it was too depressing for an entertainment show. I think they missed the whole point of the event.
- Prince and Michael Jackson failed to turn up and look how God dealt with them later in life.

The UK event finished at 10pm so we could watch a few acts from the States and still be tucked up in bed nice & early. A little-known fact is that Cliff Richard who, as some of you know, I have a love/hate* relationship with (*ok, I guess that's only half-true) was relegated to two o'clock in the morning in the BBC chat room to sing something called 'a world of difference' which the lack of an audience made into a world of indifference. Luck of the draw perhaps? Or was it that sizeable pledge from a market town in middle England on the one condition that Cliff got the graveyard slot? Moo-ha-ha.

I headed off on my gap yah as a chubby but well-groomed teenager and this is how I ended up when I got back to Europe from my travels. The jeans hadn't been washed in several weeks, the espadrills were stitched together (badly) with an M&S face cloth and the scarf was a desperate throw-back to a New Romantic era which had long-since slipped away. I was also several sizes smaller which surely made me a potential recipient of Famine Relief for the Hungry (I was absolutely starving I assure you).

There used to be a quality threshold for beards in the 80s and mine fell far short and so I was forced to shave it off. They've junked this social ruling nowadays and, compared to the rubbish efforts today, mine looks positively luxuriant.

AT Mays were a travel agents - I've still got the bag today (we built stuff to last back then).

THINGS WE WISH WE HAD BACK THEN

Part Two: CGI

We were told in 1978 that, if we watched the Superman film, we'd believe a man could fly but, let's be honest, we weren't entirely convinced, were we? Nowadays we'd happily believe that not only could he fly but he could turn into a killer robot and have holes punched through his body too. Back then, the height of special effects was Johnny Morris making us think he could hold a conversation with a chimpanzee.

Jaws was truly terrifying ... right up until the moment when the shark clambered onto the boat to eat Quint and, as we were about to scream, we turned to our mate instead and said "actually that just looks like a giant plastic fish".

Thunderbirds used to be at the cutting edge of technical wizardry, with wires spray-painted the same colour as the background to disguise them, but today you'll get more realistic spaceships in home videos on YouTube uploaded by primary school kids.

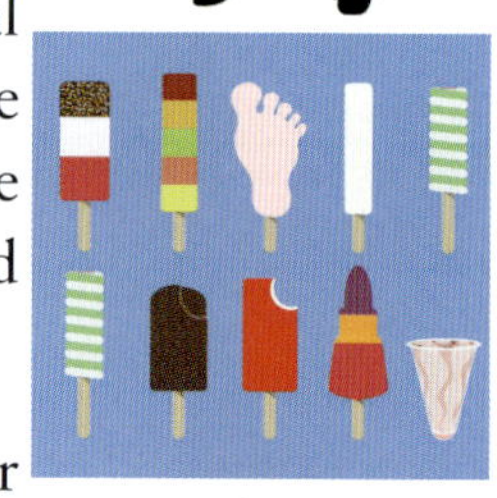

Our favourite actors now convince us they are hobbits or super-heroes or blue aliens. The Planet of the Apes reboot finally persuaded us that monkeys could ride horses and rule the world (not that those 2 things are connected – otherwise Frankie Dettori would be President of the USA). Even the BBC can make us believe that a man is actually a woman. Oh wait, hold on, that's their news reporting not their sci-fi programmes.

43 BRITISH KIDS TV (PART ONE)

The absolute very first time I remember watching what the TV industry called 'educational entertainment' was in the early 70s after I'd graduated from Watch With Mother & Play School. Once you'd reached five or six years old and had decided you were an adult, 4pm was just too childish a time slot to watch TV (although you secretly took a sneaky peek when you got home from the classroom unless, that is, you went to public school and presumably made it back to the boarding house at 7.30pm after cello practice). 5pm was when the grown-up stuff started and there was nothing more grown-up at that age than Blue Peter.

The intense rivalry for younger viewers between our two broadcasters, BBC and ITV (yes, that's right, kids, we didn't have Sky, Netflix or Disney+ but somehow managed to get through life), was epitomised by Tiswas vs Swap Shop on a Saturday morning but, in the post 5pm weekday slot, Magpie vs Blue Peter was the battleground. The BBC's flagship children's TV show was slick, with its nautical theme tune, its audience participation ranging from badges to vandalised gardens and its pets which had a habit of dying every now and then. The presenters were very professional – Valerie Singleton, Peter Purvis (fresh from Wacky Races), John Noakes & Lesley Judd were my era – and the whole thing was produced by someone called Biddy Baxter who sounded like she was the alter ego for a Marvel superhero but probably wasn't.

But it was very BBC. It was safe, comfortable, well-scripted and something our parents would approve of. Magpie, on the other hand, was improvised, edgy and a bit rough at the seams. They never pulled out 'one they'd made earlier', preferring to botch it up live instead. It was exactly the same with Tiswas & Swap Shop. Hoi polloi vs establishment. Ovett vs Coe. There was clearly a class dynamic to which station you watched (I was BBC but I'd switch to ITV when my mum was busy cooking the roast swan and my dad hadn't made it back from his game of real tennis).

The other educational entertainment programme I remember was HOW on ITV where Fred Dinenage gave us genuinely informative explanations of how things worked in down-to-earth, understandable language. It was like a kids Tomorrow's World but done in that typical unpatronising ITV style. We all loved the Native American salute when the presenters chanted HOW in unison but our kids would report them to the police nowadays for cultural appropriation.

Another BBC offer in a similar genre was Why Don't You? ('... just switch off your television set and go and do something less boring instead' to give it the full title) which helped us find things to keep us occupied during the holidays. I don't remember trying any of the boring stuff they suggested until Russell T. 'Dr Who' Davies took over as producer and told us to saw our mates in half or build a rocket and blast ourselves into space.

Here are some other classic post 5pm shows (some of them may have been a few minutes earlier – please no hate mail):

- Record Breakers – besides the McWhirter twins with their ridiculous photographic memories and Roy Castle performing 'Dedication' at the end of the show, the thing I remember most was Roy's own record-breaking endeavours – from tap dancing to airplane wing walking (what??) and playing the same tune on 43 instruments in four minutes (had someone else really done 42 or did the producers just hear an anecdote about some bloke playing a few instruments consecutively and thought it sounded like a nice, easy way of securing a spot for Roy in the Guinness Book of Records?).
- Cheggars Plays Pop – here was Keith Chegwin on one of the few TV shows in which he managed to keep all his kit on. It was surprisingly good at attracting bands but was invariably the kiss of death for their song. I'm not kidding. I've seen a list of the guest slots. It's amazing how often not-many-hit wonders played their chart-topper and then followed up a few weeks later with an absolute flop – Classix Nouveaux, King, Brian & Michael of Matchstalk Men fame, Kissing the Pink, Blue Zoo, Bluebells. The Wurzels were practically the house band. I mentioned some of these in an earlier story on one-hit wonders so what on earth were they doing turning up twice on Cheggars?.
- Crackerjack – it's Friday, it's 5 to 5, it's CRACKERJACK (am I the only one who got a little fed up shouting the name loudly every time it was mentioned? I am? Fight me). It was filmed in what became Shepherds Bush Empire where I've seen plenty of excellent bands but never a game of Double Drop. Ed Stewpot Stewart was my presenter but, if you were a little older, you had Michael Aspel and, a little younger, then Stuart Francis was your guy. If you're getting on a bit, you better have a good memory because the Beeb wiped all but two of the Aspel shows whilst retaining the full Stewpot/Francis runs.

Stewpot had with him Peter Glaze and Don Maclean (no, not the bloke who sang Bye Bye Miss American Pie). Stuart Francis, on the other hand, drew the short straw and got the Krankies, one of whom (I'm not sure which) could apparently crush a grape. It was jumble of a show with songs, comedy and some sort of improv play at the end. There were also games where the prizes were pencils. Typical, tight-fisted BBC but it was our money they were spending so I shouldn't complain. You'd rely on them back then not to waste even a few bob on a Diversity Department let alone several million pounds … although they probably needed one a lot more then than they do today.

And so, back to Blue Peter. I approached this story fully intending to give them a roasting. However, all my preconceptions have just been destroyed by one video which I'll add a link to at the bottom. It's not the one of Lulu, the defecating and urinating elephant (and before fans of the Scottish ginger singer give me any grief, I really am referring to an actual elephant). And it's not the one of Simon Groom presenting us with two examples of medieval door furniture and describing them as a beautiful pair of knockers.

No, this is the one of John 'Get down Shep' Noakes scaling Nelson's Column on a rickety ladder tied to the masonry by some old bits of rope, with no safety harness, wearing flared jeans and cracking jokes as the ladder bends backwards at the top to get over the plinth. That is genuinely the most terrifying thing I've ever seen and I've watched Dr Who & the Weeping Angels while sitting <u>on</u> not <u>behind</u> the settee. On the website, there's a warning that the video 'contains behaviour which could be imitated' although they might have added 'but you'd have to be a complete nutter to do so.'

We've got so used to health & safety rules and wrapping everyone in cotton wool that we forget that, in our day, a kids programme (and a BBC one at that) would routinely force its presenters to do something life-threatening like this. Noakesy, respect to you.

Google 'BBC archive Noakes scales Nelson's column' and be amazed.

44 BRITISH KIDS TV (PART TWO)

The absolute very first time I wrote about British Kids TV in the 70s & 80s was in the previous story, Part One, so here (predictably I know) is Part Two. The focus this time is on animation and puppetry where, compared to the slick stuff coming over from the States, British creatives brought their own unique idiosyncratic approach by which I mean quirky characters, dodgy production values and some distinctly dubious double entendres.

I'll steer clear of Saturday morning TV, Play School and Magic Roundabout because I've covered them in earlier stories (Magic Roundabout being the most popular of the ones I published on the website ... which tells me a great deal about you lot) and will focus on some other Great British classics instead.

In our culture wars with the States (yes, I know, but I'm using 'culture' in the broadest sense to include all aspects of the entertainment industry so it's not as daft a concept as it sounds), they were the kings of cartoons and, despite stiff competition from the Muppets & Sesame Street, we had the ascendancy when it came to puppets and soft toys.

We covered every base: glove puppets (a bloke called Ivan had his hand up Basil Brush – and possibly Mr Derek and Mr Roy too – whilst Harry Corbett's brother operated Sooty, Soo & Sweep), knee-sitting birds (Emu & Orville – no better advocates for the abolition of the RSPB), socks which moved by stop-animation and lived on the moon (the Clangers along with Soupdragon which happened to be what we called the vicar's wife when we were younger because of a truly uncanny resemblance) and then that saggy old cloth cat, Bagpuss, who, not so long ago apparently, could be found in "an unusual shop which didn't sell anything" (a sort of olden day WH Smiths).

We then got ones so big that they ended up being costumes for actors to wear which led to Bernie Clifton riding an orange ostrich across the Crackerjack stage and the Wombles performing on TOTP when they weren't picking up litter on Wimbledon Common, highlighting an environmental conscience long before Greta Thunberg started turning up on our TV screens.

Greta and her mates love to blame earlier generations for impending climate catastrophe but our green creds in the 70s & 80s were surprisingly good. Remember, our milk carts were electric vehicles long before hybrid cars came along (not only saving the planet but avoiding waking people up early in the morning too). We carried our shopping out of the supermarket in brown paper not plastic bags and we wrapped our dinner in newspaper once, having left the car at home, we'd walked to the chippy to pick it up. In fact, that was how we got to school too unless we rode our bikes. We turned our electricity off for a couple of hours most evenings (not always voluntarily I grant you – particularly during the winter of discontent) and for a small reward we recycled all our (glass not plastic) bottles, not via some carbon-hungry mechanical process but by paying someone to wash them up. And we're the ones who've fucked the planet?

When it came to trains (evil coal-burning ones I'm afraid), we were spoilt for choice. There was Ivor The Engine voiced by Oliver 'Bagpuss' Postgate (who even did the puffing sounds too) and then along came Ringo Starr's Thomas The Tank Engine and his Fat Controller. Even to this day, there's a heated debate amongst locomotive aficionados as to which was the superior programme. I found this well-considered argument on a railway buff's website (I've not got it bookmarked, I was just surfing the net for research purposes, honest!): 'Thomas, on the other hand, is populated by sociopathic little shits in engine form based on a nasty, rigid Little England morality that borders on medieval.' Nice to see the Welsh getting passionate about something other than sport and singing.

Our animation was generally a little more, well, basic than the US versions. Mr Benn could've been drawn in our primary school classroom and what on earth was Bod? I couldn't work out if this little bald chap was 3 or 83 (he's like Stewie from Family Guy). It's impossible not to rewatch the episodes without reaching the conclusion that the creative team were clearly smoking something at the time.

Danger Mouse was a cartoon about a secret service rodent saving the world from a tyrannical toad and a vampire duck. Sounds like some more wacky baccy here too. It was on ITV which meant, with their healthy advertising revenues in the days when people actually watched TV, they put some decent money into the production values. It was good enough to be nominated for 11 BAFTAS but didn't win one because the only award ITV ever secured was the token one patronisingly 'voted for by you the viewer.'

Penfold was voiced by Terry Scott and Danger Mouse by June Whitfield … oh no, wait, it was David Jason. Each show needed 2000 drawings which took ages to produce and cost a fortune so check out how many times there's a black-out or a snow-storm with just DM's eyes showing – it was the go-to sequence when they were running behind schedule or above budget.

Whilst I have a soft spot for many of the US cartoons – Top Cat, Wacky Races et al – I love the fact our British sense of humour meant we slipped a few adult references into the shows made over here to keep both the children and their parents entertained. I mentioned the drug-taking references and anti-French sentiment in the Magic Roundabout story but I've just seen a couple of episodes of Roobarb & Custard, the wobbly animation show where the cat's called Custard but is pink, the trees look suspiciously like hairy testicles and they refer to something called a 'furry triangle'. I'm not making this up. I'd love to think the same was true of Captain Pugwash but, sadly, Master Bates and Seaman Staines actually were made up. And Roger the Cabin Boy wasn't even an actual character let alone an instruction.

But this subtle adult humour in kids TV was nothing compared to the little-known Xmas tradition in the TV industry of the 70s whereby BBC & ITV production teams would create private videos of some of the most popular shows of the time, featuring out-takes and original material, to play at their own and each other's Xmas parties in an informal contest to see who'd produced the best. It was like the truce on the Western Front with the footie game on Xmas Day. There are a couple of absolute pearlers from Rainbow and Tom Baker's Dr Who. You really do need to watch them both just so you believe me when I talk about the innuendo and smuttiness which was always bubbling just under the surface when the Brits did kids TV in the good old days.

So, to watch Bungle & co discussing Zippy's 'big red wanger' and listen to Jane boasting about banging Rod & Roger the previous night, type 'Rainbow kids rude programme' into YouTube. For Tom Baker as Dr Who flirting drunkenly with Romana and, er, that metal dog K9, 'Dr Doug Who Tom Baker Xmas 1978' should do the trick.

45 CHOCOLATE BARS & BISCUITS

The absolute very first time I ate a wagon wheel was at a friend's party when I was six or seven years old. I wasn't offered it – I just stole it from the biscuit tin when everyone else was playing musical chairs – but it was a big as a frisbee and took so long to eat that I was caught red-handed by the host's mum.

I wasn't allowed any birthday cake as a result but cakes in those days weren't shaped like caterpillars or filled with cookie dough & chocolate pieces so I wasn't too bothered. There's only so much excitement a Victoria sponge and a few candles can generate ... especially when they're accidentally blown out before the birthday girl gets to do it. Revenge is sweet.

The manufacturers were called Burtons Gold Medal Biscuits and I worked there when I grew up. By then, I'm pretty sure wagon wheels had shrunk since that first time I'd eaten them although, to be fair, I no longer played with a frisbee nor had the hands of a seven year old (just the sense of humour apparently) so couldn't be sure. They used to be staples of the school lunchbox before the government passed a law which said they had to be replaced by an apple. By the time it was my job to sell them to the Great British Public though, I think I ate more of them off the production line than I actually managed to flog to Tesco.

Penguins were made in Manchester by United Biscuits and I worked for them too (are you sensing a theme to my career choices?). We'd got Derek Nimmo to tell kids to "p-p-p-pick up a Penguin" – well, actually we just said "pick up a penguin" but he put on his stammering vicar impression and we didn't have the heart to stop him. Club was the big competitor, made by Jacobs for people who were keen on joining a club and liked a lot of chocolate on their biscuit. They eventually started putting less of it on and soon found out that people were a little more interested in the chocolate than the club.

I was never a big fan of Milky Bars (I had a sweet tooth but these were off the scale) but how many of us knew some boy at school who was short with fair hair and glasses, probably with the frames held together by Sellotape, and so was nominated as the classroom Milky Bar kid? In our defence, it really was hard to avoid the adverts with the little geek in the cowboy outfit who told us the milky bars were on him so often that we wished the next ad in the series would include a red Indian with a sharp tomahawk.

We soon aspired to an altogether more grown-up chocolate-loving gunslinger though; the one who looked like a cartoon Clint Eastwood in the spaghetti westerns and spent most of his time biting through the chocolate on his Texan bar and chewing reeeeeaaal slow ("A last request, gringo?" "Guess I'll just finish this here chewy Texan bar"). Yes, we got the message: it was very chewy and lasted for ages … although if it was still around today, I bet I could get through it in less than 60 seconds, even if it took half my teeth out at the same time.

In the 70s & 80s, when the only Galaxy you ever wanted came in a foil wrapper and couldn't connect to the internet, Birmingham-based Cadbury became the No.1 chocolate-maker by first getting Frank Muir to tell us we were all fruit & nutcases and then teaching the whole country to chant "nuts whole hazelnuts UH" at each other.

Nestles, which rhymed with 'wrestles' until we joined the Common Market and were forced by EU law to call them Nestlé instead, tried to take advantage of our membership by sending truckloads of Swiss chocolate over the border. In solidarity with our Brummie confectioners, we sent them all back again claiming not to like foreign chocolate (we kept the Milky Bars as a friendly gesture) but they had the last laugh by buying our Rowntree Mackintosh factories and selling us Kit Kat instead. We knew when we were beaten.

Cadbury tried fighting back by coming up with adverts for Caramel which featured a sexy bunny and her beaver (to clarify, that's another cartoon character, as in "hey, Mr Beaver, why are you beavering around"). Despite the weird West Country accent, I always pictured her as Raquel Welch (if Raquel lived in Yeovil rather than LA) but I've just found out she was voiced by Miriam Margolyes which puts a rather different complexion on things.

For nut-lovers, there was Topic with its hazelnut in every bite (yes, I know, 'just like squirrel poo'). Other options included Banjo (previously Trophy) and Marathon until Mars, who produced both bars, played a sick joke on us by first discontinuing Banjo and then changing the name of Marathon to Snickers, just so they could save money by rehashing the adverts from the States. It meant the end of those British ads with the dance troupe who had the letters of the brand spelt out on the tops of the guys & girls as they ran around a giant model of the bar. Sadly, they moved around so much that they rarely spelled Marathon correctly – in fact I'm sure there's a moment when 'R' disappears behind the giant bar with 'A HOT MAN' charging after her (yes, I know, I'm sorry and you're right ... very ashamed).

My mum believed in good old-fashioned home-cooked food (no Vesta curries for me) which meant, if you declined second and third helpings, you were basically saying it tasted disgusting so you tended to shut up and eat up. From some reason though, she also had a cupboard full of chocolate bars and I was allowed three every afternoon when I got back from school (Double Decker, Turkish Delight and Treets which were deliberately mis-spelt to mess with kids' heads and piss off their teachers). This daily calorie intake coupled with multiple helpings of dinner would've made a little fatty out of me nowadays but, back then, I was expected to go up to the playing fields for a few hours everyday after school and burn it all off. If it wasn't pitch black by the time I staggered home exhausted and ready for a bath (we didn't have showers in those days and we'd certainly never heard of shower gel), my mum would turn me round at the door and send me back out again.

With that in mind, forgive me for questioning the government's response to rising obesity levels in children which basically consists of treating sweets, crisps and chocolate as though they were cigarettes and trying to penalise kids for eating them. Wouldn't it be better to encourage them just to exercise a little more instead?

So look, here's the answer for the parents, teachers and law-makers of today. If those sneaky buggers at Burtons keep shrinking your wagon wheels, only buy them on BOGOF and hand one back for a refund. Force schools to dress the kids up with letters on their tops and make them dance round a giant chocolate bar – this helps with their spelling too. Encourage games of cowboys & indians and nominate the least fit child as the Milky Bar Kid so they get the most exercise being chased around the playing field. Don't let them do anything reeeeeaaal slow and never criticise them for beavering around. Lastly, advise them against working for a biscuit company when they grow up – the pay's crap and the perks are fattening.

46 XMAS MEMORIES

The absolute very first time I must've heard about Father Christmas was in the late 60s when I was a toddler. The second time was the following year when my brother, who was quite a bit older than me, told me that Santa didn't exist and our chimney was clogged up with broken roofing tiles and dead birds so nobody could inch their way down it anyway. Also, reindeer couldn't fly and Icelandic people ate them. Possibly as a direct consequence.

In those days, we were happy to find pictures of nativity scenes behind the windows of our advent calendars rather than some trinket from Louis Vuitton which wouldn't seem out of place in a goodie bag at the Oscars. We never got garage-loads of presents and nor did our stockings look like they were Hattie Jacques' hand-me-downs. Instead, they were actual socks – usually short ones we'd grown out of three years earlier – and only big enough to hold some chocolate money and an orange (and not a nice choccy one from Terrys but a real one which mum had bought from Gateway or Fine Fare several weeks earlier).

My kids have grown up now but, like us when we were young, they used to jump on our bed shockingly early on Xmas morning to open their stocking presents. That's where the similarities ended though as the small socks of our youth had turned into industrial-sized sacks which they struggled to drag through the door. I'd nearly wrecked my back the previous night lifting them onto their beds as I tiptoed into their rooms after midnight trying not to disturb them. They were wide awake though, pausing from their Nintendo DS to video me so they could prove that Santa didn't exist if, at any time in the future, I tried to bribe them into behaving themselves with any claim to the contrary.

The gifts themselves had increased in size (and cost) as well. The only way our kids would've accepted the sort of stuff we were given when we were younger was if the orange was a type of mobile phone and the money wasn't chocolate but legal tender, preferably in high denomination banknotes.

Back in the old days, we had to wait for Dad to fetch my grandparents before we could open our presents under the tree (both of them … and one was a book). We could've got stuck in far earlier if Nana & Grandpa had got a taxi or hitched or not turned up at all although that would've deprived us of their not-so-silent but deadly farts at the dinner table, drawing a slap from Mum if we weren't able to stifle a laugh – for us not them, just to be clear, although it would've been far fairer if they'd been the ones to get a clip round the ear instead.

It was tough for Dad to distribute the presents because they tended to be covered by a sightscreen of tinsel. My mum always insisted on getting a real Xmas tree and then obscuring it with so much decoration that you wouldn't know it wasn't artificial anyway (until it toppled under the weight and fell onto the stereo system which was the name we gave to our version of the iPhone in the 70s & 80s).

Once we'd unwrapped our book, clearly the second present was the big one. For me, I was hoping for either Subbuteo or one of the Action

Man figures, ideally with realistic hair and gripping hands. Instead, I'd often get a) a second book, b) something which belonged to my older brother or sister or, if I'd presumably been the world's naughtiest child, c) a book belonging to my older brother and sister.

We were then given a couple of hours to play with our presents which was ample time because there was only so much fun you could get out of an orange, some reading material and a bit of money in the days before our pop stars managed to figure out something more exciting.

In the meantime, an army of people invaded our house to get pissed. Dad always managed to secure two pins (80 pints) of Abbot Ale at Xmas (we never asked him where from but he was a member of the rugby club and those lads could lift a few barrels pretty quickly if the landlord of the pub was unexpectedly called to the telephone). Abbot had an ABV of 5% but this was effectively doubled if consumed before midday so, as more people arrived, I was often called on for bar-tender duties. I was nine when I was trusted to fill up the tankards and 12 when I was allowed (ok, encouraged) to take a sip myself. Quality parenting.

Lunches around my home town were postponed, sometimes indefinitely, as our house shook to the mis-remembered lyrics of Any Old Iron and anything by Ray Conniff or the Black & White Minstrels (the less said about them the better – I tell my kids they were a fictitious rumour dreamed up by the woke brigade).

Once most of the stragglers had gone (including one chap who'd only knocked on the door to ask for directions to his cousin's house – true story), it was time for lunch … or supper as it was called by then. We had a Hostess heated trolley which needed to make the journey between the kitchen and the dining room over shag carpets and several rugs. It was a tricky obstacle course at the best of times but, after several pints of Abbot, it became virtually impassable. We actually had a serving hatch between the two rooms which would have been far easier and quicker to negotiate but Mum and Dad had saved up several books of

Green Shield Stamps to buy the Hostess trolley so we had to make full use out of it.

After the Xmas pud – full of such low value coins that, even if one of us had eaten the whole thing on our own, we'd only have collected enough cash to buy a couple of Banjo bars – and the obligatory arguments (usually over helping with the washing up which, in those dishwasher-less days, was worse than hard labour), we would settle down to a board game in the evening. Originally, it was Totopoly or Cluedo before we moved on to more cerebral challenges like Pictionary and Trivial Pursuit where it was wise to avoid partnering with Dad once the Abbot had made him more interested in playing with the cheese wedges on the board than helping his young son answer some obscure question on the Suez Crisis.

Looking back, it's interesting how many of these traditions I've introduced to my own family years later ... whilst obviously improving on a couple. Dad had a decent system for distribution of the presents, ensuring the best was dished out last, but much as I approved of the general principle behind his approach, the execution was frankly a little on the amateurish side. Once I had children of my own, I developed a far more professional process with all the gift tags colour-coded and numbered to ensure an Amazon-efficient logistics exercise. I'm genuinely not joking. My kids think I'm weird but I bet, when it comes to their turn, they'll be the ones copying my approach and, almost certainly, I'll be the one farting at the dinner table.

Here's the photo which Rob based his illustration off. It must've been before I was born so we had to photoshop me in. Either that or my folks didn't want me in the shot.

47 SCOOBY DOO

The absolute very first time I saw Scooby Doo was in the early 70s when it was just a cartoon rather than a set of distinctly average live-action films starring the girl from Buffy the Vampire Slayer. Also, in my day, there was only one dog and it certainly wasn't an irritating little yappy thing called Scrappy which made you long for a guest appearance from Cruella de Vil and that dognapping van of hers.

Scooby Doo was named after Frank Sinatra's scatting at the end of Strangers in the Night. I've just listened to the song (after googling what 'scatting' meant) and thank goodness they didn't pick Da Da Da Da Da Di-Ya instead, for several reasons not least of which was it didn't actually rhyme with 'Where Are You?'.

Apparently, Scooby was a Great Dane (who knew?) but, with his brown fur and black spots, he looked like a weird cross-breed of Dalmatian and Rottweiler. He talked but, let's be honest, pretty bloody badly. I could never understand much of what he said although "Rooby-Rooby-Roo" seemed to be his catchphrase, often followed by a Muttley laugh (and there is no catchphrase in the history of television which can't be improved by the addition of a Muttley laugh). Just as often we'd get "Ruh-roh, Raggy" when the shit really hit the fan which is what shit tends to do when a group of young people make the unusual decision not to go to the pub but head for, say, an abandoned mineshaft instead.

His best friend (or owner?) was a hippy called Shaggy who had a habit of wearing a green t-shirt & brown cords and shouting "Zoinks". He was either aspergers or a pot-head. Judging by the flower-power psychedelic van, I suspect the latter which would mean he joins Dylan from Magic Roundabout as another drug-taking role model for us impressionable kids in the 70s.

Their gang was called Mystery Inc (which I always assumed was a form of secret writing they used to solve cases) and the show was based on four young people and a dog investigating a series of mysteries. Hmmm, didn't Enid Blyton do exactly the same thing in the UK decades earlier with the Famous Five? Two girls, two boys and a dog named Timmy/Scooby (I always thought the Frank Sinatra story sounded questionable). Substitute a few scooby snacks for lashings of ginger beer and it's clear that Hanna & Barbera lifted the whole idea off our Enid. And the end result? 50 years after she died, Enid is now forgotten, cancelled for her politically-incorrect stories (presumably Noddy and Big Ears weren't gay enough), whilst, on the other side of the pond, Scooby & Co are Hollywood royalty instead.

The leader of the gang was Fred (no doubt because he wore a cravat – fine for a gap-toothed old cad like Terry-Thomas but not the most obvious choice for a hip young bloke in the 70s) who spent every episode getting hypnotised or setting traps for the various monsters & ghosts which Scooby & Shaggy would almost certainly end up setting off themselves. This was partly because Fred would always suggest the team split up to hunt their target and, for some inexplicable reason, would plump for the combination – Scooby & Shaggy – most likely to muck things up. He sometimes sent Velma with them too though, presumably so he could be alone with Daphne and take her up the dark passageway without the others seeing.

Like most boys my age (by which I mean back then not now), I had quite a soft spot for accident-prone Daphne with her purple dress and green scarf. In fact, I fancied any female cartoon character who was remotely sexy – Penelope Pitstop, Jessica Rabbit, the bunny off the Caramel adverts and Wilma Flintstone who reminded me of my teacher (if my teacher wore a pearl necklace and a shredded white dress which, sadly, she only did in my dreams and not while making us practice our times tables).

The odd one was Velma (I always thought she was called Thelma – as in Louise's mate – who on earth has heard of Velma as a name?). She used to wear an orange chunky jumper with matching knee length socks, short skirt and glasses which was an outfit full of mixed signals. Invariably, her glasses would be knocked off during some chase scene which meant she tended to spend most of the episode crawling around on all fours looking for them. She's just being rebooted as a gender-fluid lesbian of Asian origin without her orange outfit for a new HBO show which takes place in a universe where Scooby and the others don't exist. Er, is it just me but what's the point in calling her Velma then?

Apparently, their full names were revealed at some point as Norville 'Shaggy' Rogers, Daphne Blake, Fred Jones and Velma Dinkley (they really had it in for her didn't they – she's clearly the one who all the producers and writers hated, just like Play School's Hamble).

I'm not sure if Scooby's surname was Doo or whether he had one of those double-barrelled first names like Sarah Jane off Dr Who but both he and Shaggy clearly had some sort of eating disorder which meant they were permanently hungry and so were easily coerced by the others, with bribes of Scooby snacks or giant sandwiches, to do something they didn't really want to (a useful life lesson which many of us kids put into practice in the school playground). They also had a tendency to ride unicycles a lot which were clearly more common on American roads than they were over here because I only ever saw them in US cartoons on the telly and never wheeling past me as I trudged to school on a damp winter morning in the UK.

No one could argue that the Mystery Inc team weren't highly successful – nearly 90 cases in the original run (by which I mean the episodes before Scrappy Doo and his Puppy Power made an unwelcome entry in 1979 – there's a smutty joke there somewhere but I won't demean myself, or you, by going for it) and a 100% success rate in crime-solving which would be the envy of any police force or detective agency in the world. In fact, those stats are matched only by … wait for it … the Famous Five. Told you. Her estate should sue for royalties.

If only they'd been patrolling the streets of the UK instead of the American Wild West or wherever it was they patrolled (clearly somewhere with an abundance of haunted houses, ghost towns, mineshafts and abandoned amusement arcades anyway) because we could've asked them to unmask the criminals who vandalised the Blue Peter garden. I'd love to have seen them rip the Les Ferdinand mask off the perpetrator (we never really believed that one did we, despite his admission of guilt – no doubt secured under duress) to reveal John Noakes telling us he'd have got away with it if it wasn't for those meddling kids and a slightly sheepish Shep muttering "Ruh-roh, Raggy" behind him.

48 FREE TIME

The absolute very first time I went to the fair was in the mid 70s when I was old enough to be short-changed by the guy on the dodgems and mugged by the hook-a-duck lady as I made my way home (I was pretty inexperienced then but at least I think she was mugging me). I ate so much candy floss and so many toffee apples that I was violently sick which is a pretty anti-social thing to do if you're on the Big Wheel at the time though I suppose it would've been even worse on the waltzers.

In the days before instant entertainment on mobile phones, computers & satellite TV channels, we had to work hard in the 70s & 80s to make the most of our free time … which was often considerable because schools in those days tended not to put on the countless after-school clubs which allow parents to go out to the pub, grab a donner kebab on the way back and still get home before their kids. Instead, you'd be kicked out onto the streets soon after lunch once the teacher taking the final lesson had got too bored to carry on. There was no such thing as pick-up time anyway. You walked home. It gave you a far better chance of getting into trouble on the way.

Finishing so early meant our primary leisure activities tended to be outdoors. It was our naive old-fashioned way of avoiding child obesity but we've obviously developed far more sophisticated strategies since then like trying to ban kids from eating Hula Hoops and drinking Coke – ingenious. We'd play 'jumpers for goalposts' games of footie, do wheelies on our Raleigh Chopper bikes, hop & jump our way up the hopscotch grid and back again, launch ourselves between two whirling skipping ropes and bounce up & down on big orange space hoppers (which admittedly could be done indoors as well but it was far more exciting to try it on the road outside your house especially if, like me, you lived on a hill).

I also went through a phase of building balsa wood planes and taking them up the 'Rec' to try them out on the boating lake and, if you're wondering how you try out balsa wood planes on a boating lake, you've clearly never loaded them up with gravel and used a strong elastic band to send them over the shipping lanes in kamikaze raids. We didn't have safe spaces in those days so, if you took your brand-new model ship up to the Rec and it was bombed less than a minute after you'd placed it carefully on the side of the lake and pushed it gently towards the middle, then you only had yourself to blame.

Back then, you couldn't text anyone to see if they were free and you only had one telephone (that's what we called the landline) which your older sister would almost certainly be using all evening. So, if you wanted to check if your mates could come out to play, you had to bike round to their house and ring the doorbell, hoping that their mum would answer the door and not their dad who tended to ask you highly inappropriate questions about your own mum.

If there was torrential rain (a shower wasn't severe enough in those days for our parents to call us back in), we'd have to find things to do indoors instead. Like the telephone, there was only one TV in the house and so we could only ever watch what the whole family wanted to. In my home, this usually meant period dramas (Poldark, Upstairs Downstairs) rather than cop shows (Sweeney, Professionals, Starsky &

Hutch and 'who loves ya, baby' Kojak) so it was a relief when Atari came out with their home video game systems (remember that tennis game with the amazing true-to-life graphics?) for us to play in the comfort of our bedroom … until we realised that we had to connect it up to the TV set and so were in the same dilemma as before, competing with the Onedin Line which, as far as mum was concerned, was a losing battle right from the outset.

We didn't know at the time but this was the start of a slippery slope which would take us from family nights watching TV together via Atari tennis contests with our parents and then the odd game of Pac Man in our local cafe or chip shop right through to the anti-social behaviour of teenagers today who lock themselves in their bedrooms for several weeks at a time, refusing to engage with the outside world until they've managed to work out how to defeat the toad-like creature which is blocking their progression to the next level of Artemis Halo Death Stalker 6.

When there was a TV programme we didn't want to watch (highly likely in the 70s & early 80s with only three channels available, one of which was BBC2) we'd read instead. Admittedly, this often meant comics & magazines – Beano & Dandy, Jackie & Mandy, Smash Hits – which were meant to be delivered with our newspapers by WH Smiths (they used to write our address on the cover just to stop us from cutting out the picture and blu-tacking it onto our bedroom wall) but usually ended up in a hedge at the bottom of the street after the paper boy had finished reading them.

We'd always be sent to bed far earlier than kids that age today (who throw a wobbly if they're asked politely to head upstairs any time before midnight) but at least we'd be allowed to read a book for 20 minutes or so. My favourite stories were Stig of the Dump, the Narnia series and anything by Roald Dahl. I still think that Charlie and the Chocolate Factory is the only book I've ever read twice, assuming that 50 Shades of Grey doesn't count. I tried reading the BFG when I was a bit older too but only because I thought it stood for something dirty.

Another alternative to the telly was playing board games which, unlike domestic pets in the 70s & 80s, weren't just for Xmas. We'd often have a cheeky game of Scrabble when Dad came home from work which was most fun on the nights when he'd had a few beers beforehand and would forget how to spell words like 'tanker' and 'rugger' which my older sister and brother would find terribly funny and our mum would get very upset about for some reason.

Looking back on this topic, I'm amazed at how many activities we found to keep us occupied in the old days (I've missed tons I know – playing kiss chase with our Action Man & Barbie dolls, treading on subbuteo figures, swapping Brooke Bond tea cards, throwing sticks into chestnut trees for conkers, earning bronze/silver/gold patches to sew onto our swimsuits) but also how many of them we did with our family and friends rather than on our own.

And, now the kids are off our hands, work's starting to ease off and we're getting ready to enjoy all this free time again for the first time since our youth, we could do a lot worse than dust off the scrabble, head down to the boating lake with our balsa wood planes (if either of these still exist), grab our sick bags for a spin on the waltzers or dig out our old space hoppers for a bounce down the nearest hill. We might want to give footie, hopscotch and skipping a miss though – I'm not sure the knees are up to it anymore. Same with the hook-a-duck lady to be honest.

Someone on FB reminded me about 'hedge-hopping' which I'd left out of the story because I didn't think anyone else did it. We called it 'garden-hopping' and, as teenagers, we would run down the length of an entire street (usually Tinwell Rd) in the small hours via the back gardens. There were no security lights in those days and fences tended to be low so that neighbours could actually talk to each other rather than send one another abusive emails. That said, one night we were accosted by an owner with a torch demanding to know what we were doing there at two o'clock in the morning. Instead of asking him exactly the same thing, we legged it and I remember clambering over a very high back wall and plummeting down the other side just as my mate burst through the gate below and ran straight through. I cling on to the hope that we'd interrupted a burglary and that the real owner was eternally grateful to 'those plucky lads'… but I doubt it somehow.

49 CARRY ON FILMS

The absolute very first time I saw a Carry On film was probably on telly in the 70s. I'm pretty sure it was 'Up the Khyber' which, at the time, I may not have realised was cockney rhyming slang and, to be fair, I probably wouldn't have understood it even if I did. I remember my older sister laughing at the name but let's hope that was because she was studying Central Asian geopolitics at the time.

The Carry On films were quintessentially-British, created by UK production teams at Pinewood Studios, featuring home-grown actors & local locations and aimed fairly & squarely at a domestic audience who found humour in everyday situations but particularly those which involved going to the toilet. There were no token Hollywood actresses to appeal cynically to the cinema-going public across the pond (you know who you are Richard 'Four Weddings/Notting Hill' Curtis) and the films weren't trying to make a social statement or lecture us on how to behave – they were just trying to make us laugh. I know, naive or what?

Our folks had several years of the franchise under their belts but young kids growing up in the 70s were totally unprepared for the Carry On innuendo. The raunchiest stuff we'd seen on telly before then was Brian Cant flirting with Toni Arthur on Play School, Florence hitting on Dylan in Magic Roundabout and John Noakes, Peter Purves & Valerie Singleton … well, let's not go into what they got up to once the Blue Peter cameras stopped rolling.

The Carry On franchise has now been firmly consigned to the culture dustbin by today's liberal elite who, thankfully, are helping us hoi polloi work out what we're allowed to watch – we simply can't be trusted otherwise and it would be carnage. I sneakily saw a few re-runs fairly recently (I closed the lounge curtains and turned the volume down, obviously). They were Cleo, Screaming, Nurse, Khyber and Camping (yes I know, a dose of COVID gave me a little more free time than I was expecting). I think I may have been committing a non-crime hate crime – whatever one of those is – so I'm relying on you not to spill the beans (which, according to the Beano's Bash Street Kids, is what all school children did or didn't do in the 70s).

To be fair, we've all been conditioned to believe that the films were several degrees worse than 'video nasties' (which used to be horrific enough to be the target of a Daily Mail campaign but are now considered so mundane that they're just called 'videos') and I was expecting a torrent of misogynistic jibes but was surprised at how many of the jokes were either aimed at the blokes or were simply bad puns.

- "You stood on my Indian dress". "Sari." "Don't mention it".
- "Somebody tried to shoot me in the Schnitzelstrasse" "Oh, that sounds painful".
- "Professor is injured. Is bleeding terrible" "Never mind his qualifications, is he hurt badly?"
- "Do you mind if I smoke?" "Not at all" (Fenella Fielding's vampire then gently combusts)

- “Your rank?” “Well, that’s a matter of opinion”
- “Infamy infamy, they’ve all got it infamy”
- “I’m taking this cow to the bull” “Couldn’t your father do it?” “No, it must be the bull”
- “Doctor, please I want to be wooed” “You can be as wude as you like”

It was actually the James Bond films at the time (in the days before 007 got in touch with his feminine side and grew a social conscience about killing and shagging) which had far more suggestive exchanges. “I’m Plenty O’Toole” “Named after your father perhaps?” or “My name is Pussy Galore” “I must be dreaming”. In fact, if you didn’t know the Bond references, you’d probably have guessed they were Carry On quotes. The actual names which Sid & the gang took on were far tamer though: Dr Tinkle, Private Widdle, Khasi of Kalabar, WC Boggs (he ran a toilet manufacturers). The nearest they got to the racy Bond character names were Dr Nookey and Arthur Upmore, bless them.

This time round, I may not have cried with laughter as I did when I first saw the films but they brought back happy memories of watching them together with the whole family (I’ve told you before – one telly, three channels, no choice) and then practising our Kenneth Williams “oh, matron” impressions and the Sid James dirty laugh. I had to work particularly hard at Sid’s cackle because I tended to come over a bit Muttley. Mum, on the other hand, got it down to a tee which in hindsight is more than a little disconcerting.

Watching them again reminded me of those unenlightened days when we’d chuckle at things which were mildly offensive rather than report them to the police and roar with laughter at the ridiculous attempts Bernard Bresslaw and Sid James made to find a way to sneak into women-only spaces like changing rooms and dorms, little knowing how much easier that would become just a few decades later.

Apparently, I've been to many of the production locations without even realising it because they had to be within a minibus ride of the Pinewood Studio complex near Slough (to save a few bob rather than the planet but at least that celeb generation didn't fly around in private jets and then lecture us on cutting our carbon emissions). A park in Gerrards Cross was transformed into Ancient Rome for Cleo by adding, well, they didn't actually make any changes at all – it just looked like a park in Gerrards Cross plonked at the end of the Forum. I've also had the pleasure of a finger being introduced to a place where fingers are rarely meant to venture in the same hospital where Charles Hawtrey received similar treatment in one of the Doctor films ("oh hello" indeed).

There were 29 films released over 20 years and they made Sid, the two Kenneths, Charles, Joan, Babs, Bernard and Hattie household names. Only the last few of the releases could be described as uncomfortably smutty, not just by the Twitterati (predictably) but also by the rest of us normal folk who somehow manage to avoid sending hate mail to JK Rowling. Those ones were indeed the cinematic equivalent of some of the less subtle seaside postcards which showed buxom women complaining about police officers wielding dangerous weapons or telling off car mechanics for inspecting their rear ends.

By that time though, the franchise was well past its prime and it seems hugely unfair for critics to hold these last few up as examples of the entire genre. You can almost hear that nasal whine from the grave of Kenneth Williams – if his ashes weren't scattered over East Finchley crematorium that is – crying "infamy, infamy they've all got it infamy".

A very helpful commentator on Facebook (there are lots of them out there) saw Rob's illustration and pointed out that it was Kenneth Williams not Frankie who said the classic 'Infamy' line. I often think that social media has been a mixed blessing for the world but I sometimes wonder if this is being too generous.

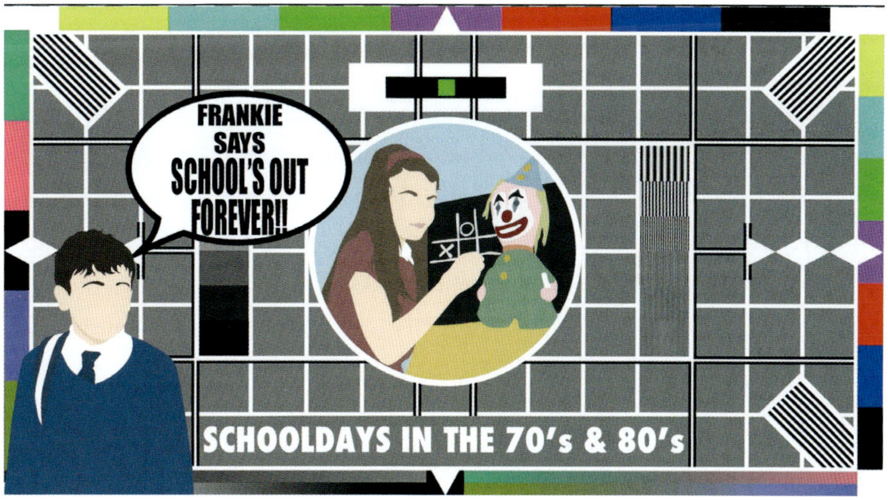

50 SCHOOLDAYS

The absolute very first time I saw a girl's knickers (as I might have mentioned before – it clearly traumatised me) was in the playground of my primary school in the early 70s. I think it cost me a fruit salad or some sherbet dip dab but I don't remember being asked to show my pants in return even though half a packet of space dust or a few spangles would probably have done the trick.

I didn't really enjoy those early school days very much. I was in a constant state of fear that my mum would forget to pack my gym kit on the days we had PE and I'd be forced to perform in my Y-Fronts (and I'm pretty sure, if that were to happen, I'd not get so much as a blackjack from my PE teacher let alone space dust or spangles).

The games of British Bulldog were equally embarrassing, especially when you'd been floored by the smallest kid in the school and could only watch helplessly as the girl who'd promised to go out with you just a couple of days earlier made alarmingly little effort to avoid the clutches of one of the sporty boys in the year above (you know who you are, Sarah).

I seem to remember breaktimes at primary school far better than I do the actual lessons. There were the games of paper fortune-teller which were meant to identify future events like who you were going to marry (which, in my case when Sarah was in charge of the game, often turned out to be the Headmaster or my mum) as well as conker contests which became so competitive that kids would bake them in the oven at home in an effort to cheat – presumably the same kids who'd grow up to be members of parliament and put in dubious expense claims for duck houses and porn films (for absolute clarity, I think these were on separate occasions and not part of the same claim – that really would've been weird).

When we moved up to the secondary school, the levels of bullying, sarcasm and ritual humiliation went up a few notches ... although this was mainly from the teachers now to be fair. We had one who would draw chalk circles on his blackboard at the beginning of the lesson and punish pupils by making them stand at the front with their nose in one of the rings when they did something wrong. It was an odd punishment because it encouraged you to misdemean early so that you could pick one of the more accessible circles (the worst were at six feet and six inches) but that was largely academic (not literally) because the purpose of the exercise was purely to provide an anecdote for the teacher to tell his mates down the pub later that day (which meant lunchtime in his case).

Another form of torture, less subtle and bordering on GBH, created a real buzz in the staff room at break-time as league tables were updated with the results of how many pupils the teachers had managed to hit with the wooden blackboard dusters. Extra points were awarded for a perfect chalk rectangle on the blazer. You'd often be summoned to the staff room under the pretext of handing in your prep early just so they could check one of the claims.

And was mine the only school where the science teachers used to lie stretched out on the lab bench in front of the Bunsen burners and answer any "excuse me, sir" enquiry with "why, what have you done?" whilst looking very pleased with themselves? Why did teaching attract such weirdos in our day? Besides the sadists in our school, there was the odd hunchback plus the one who looked like a weeble (those egg-shaped toys which wobbled but didn't fall down ... unless you used a hammer) and who would wear shorts & long white socks as soon as the temperatures rose above freezing, somehow oblivious to the fact that this made him the No.1 target for mickey-taking in the school (and not just by the pupils I assure you).

In our day, GCSEs were called O-Levels where the 'O' stood for 'Ordinary' which, let's be honest, was a little deflating whether you were successful in them or not. Our exams had proper grades (A-F and U) and were marked strictly on the basis of reflecting the pupil's ability rather than cheering them up to improve their mental health. I know, how archaic. My brother got a U in his Art O-Level for drawing a picture of a jockstrap (true story). His teacher felt he was very unlucky because it was such a realistic jockstrap ... although I couldn't help but feel that might have been part of the problem.

Punishment came in the form of lines or dates, both of which involved spending hours writing out the same thing over and over again in your exercise book and led directly to one of us inventing copy & paste when we grew up (you're welcome, kids). We also did our homework by looking through our textbooks and coming up with solutions ourselves rather than googling the answer and pressing print. It seems a bit naive now but we found it an oddly reliable way of learning the subject.

In the days before 'healthy eating' campaigns, school dinners were truly dreadful and were served to us by inmates on day release from Borstal. We'd have been delighted to receive something as nutritious as turkey twizzlers but were given roadkill with lumpy potato and even lumpier gravy instead. Nowadays, it's à la carte menus and Michelin-starred dishes with couscous, avocado and quinoa. If the potato gratin or jus is lumpy, it's because Heston Blumenthal designed it that way.

After lunch, it was games so we'd jump in the minibus and drive off to get our heads kicked in by the posh school which our headmaster insisted on us playing so he could try and get a job on their staff. The only light relief was making signs to stick to the back windscreen, saying 'smile if you did it last night.' A huge roar would go up from the whole minibus (including the teacher driving it) if we got a thumbs up from the car behind, even more so if his girlfriend was in the passenger seat at the time attempting to hide below the dashboard.

School discos were notoriously embarrassing affairs as groups of bumfluffed boys huddled together and pointed out which girls we fancied whilst having no intention whatsoever of plucking up the courage to ask them to dance. Instead, our idea of a mating ritual was to watch them sway gracefully to Soft Cell before piling onto the dancefloor and jumping around to the Jam to impress them. It's a tactic I've used on several occasions later in life but, funnily enough, with a success rate which has remained consistently and stubbornly low.

So, what's changed? If, nowadays, you offered a girl a few sweets to see her knickers in the playground, you'd be served with a restraining order and a suspended sentence. If you complained that one of your exam questions triggered some deep-rooted anxiety, you'd be awarded an A* and automatic entry to the Oxbridge college of your choice. Were you to ask car drivers to smile if they'd done it last night, they'd take a photo of you on their iPhone and have you expelled before the minibus had made it back to your school. And, although I sometimes dream that Sarah still plays British Bulldog, if she made a dash for it once I'd finally tracked her down again, I don't honestly think I've got the legs to catch her anymore.

Rob made a good point about the test card in his illustration. How on earth did the girl and the clown fail to put an O or X in the middle of the noughts & crosses grid? Absolute amateurs.

Additional Notes and Asides

- All Saints Church – you'll have read that the church played a minor but nonetheless persistent role in my early childhood. It's not as if I ever believed in a god, nor were my parents particularly religious. It's just what you did in middle England communities like mine in the 70s. I knew my days in the church choir were numbered when I was too busy working out the cricket score from the sermon (mentions of the 'Lord' = two runs, 'Jesus' = four, 'Christ' six and 'God' was out) to launch into my opening solo for the Magnificat. I've barely been back to church since but, let's be honest, I'm hardly the only one, am I?

- BBC – my word, they used to lecture us when we were younger … and they still do now that we're older which seems a bit unfair. While we were distracted with all that growing up stuff, they were quietly ditching the stiff suits and turning all young, trendy and hip without us noticing. It makes me laugh (a hollow and painful one obviously) to see how they don't mind alienating their older audience anymore as long as they win over the kids ... and yet we're the only ones still watching terrestrial telly. It's also odd how the most virtue-signalling businesses – the BBC, banks, credit card companies – are the ones which have the least reason to do so. Work that one out.

- British Bulldog – reading my stories back, I'm surprised at how often this game cropped up. I've probably mentioned it more times than I actually played it. I assume this reveals some deep-rooted anxiety, like dreams where you're being chased without your clothes on. Now, that would've made British Bulldog more interesting.

- Cartoons – it's been amazing to find out how few episodes of our favourites were actually made. Top Cat was one of the top dogs with 30 but the rest were measly: 17 for Wacky Races and the same number for the Dastardly & Muttley spin-off (which I got called out for referring to as 'Catch The Pigeon' in my original post), 16 for Hong Kong Phooey but only 13-14 for the British triumvirate of Bod, Bagpuss and Mr Benn (our animators keeping it short & sweet or, in the case of Bod, just short). Admittedly, there were 166 episodes of the Flintstones but that meant 166 opportunities to see my beloved Wilma so still too few. By the way, I now know that 'Catch The Pigeon' wasn't the name of the show but it wasn't even in the lyrics to the intro song. We all just made it up. Google it if you don't believe me.

- Dallas – my least popular post. Hardly any of you actually clicked on it originally (regardless of whether it was any good) and I'm pretty sure those that did stumbled upon it by mistake while googling a video of a similar name. I suppose JR looks positively tame compared to the scheming, manipulative bastards who've turned up on the world stage since (and, believe me, I'm not just referring to Game of Thrones).

- Films – I don't read many books twice but I've watched my favourite films (Grease, Animal House, Life of Brian, Blues Brothers) so many times that I can recite most of the dialogue, by which I mean all of it. I fully understand how irritating this can be but fortunately my family rarely listen to a word I say anyway. I used to pick up my son from primary school and tell him "we got a full tank of gas, half a pack of cigarettes, it's dark and we're wearing sunglasses". He would just look at me with a mixture of pity and disdain before asking for one of the cigarettes.

- Frankie Goes to Hollywood – I remember seeing the demo for Relax on The Tube (along with a couple of semi-naked dancing girls in bondage gear – on the TV, that is, not sitting in the lounge with me). I rewatched the video numerous times … and, before you say anything, it was because I liked the song. That's why I frequently reference FGTH's advice for us to relax if we wanted to come. Oh dear, perhaps you were right after all.

- Magic Roundabout & Play School – only 'Xmas' & 'Schooldays' could compete with these two stories for reader numbers on the website. You're such a bunch of softies.

- Pop Music – you'll have noticed how many 80s bands/songs I namecheck. I'm still living in the forlorn hope that the Smiths will reform. I saw Morrissey at a festival several years ago. I had my little girl on my shoulders and was quite drunk by the time he took to the stage but he played loads of old Smiths songs and I danced deliriously, much to my daughter's apparent delight … until my wife took her off me and pointed out she wasn't laughing but bawling her eyes out instead. For a while I was restricted to seeing her once a week and only under supervision.

- Radio DJs – my daughter watched a documentary on Jimmy Savile with me recently (that's what happens when you lift the restraining order too early) and it only dawned on her then that DJ stood for 'Disc Jockey'. They were the voice of our youth but many of them (John Peel aside) were irritating or naff or, as we've subsequently found out, far worse than that. All the DJs on Radio 1 nowadays are barely out of their teens but, in our day, they were mainly middle-aged blokes. I hate to admit it but I think the BBC may actually have got this one right for once.

- Russell T. Davies – he's not much older than us but it's incredible what he's worked on over the years: Why Don't You?, The Flashing Blade parody and Dr Who. He's had more dream jobs than Neil Tennant (and Neil's been a writer for Smash Hits, the editor of UK Marvel comics and half of a famous pop duo). The BBC have asked him to come back to Dr Who, now that they've made sure it's disappeared down the toilet. That's Russell not Neil ... although even a Pet Shop Boys' take on Dr Who might be an improvement on what they're airing nowadays.

- Social Media – what can I say? A communication marvel and the root of all evil. Just think of the shit we'd be in today if every drunken or indiscrete comment we ever made was sitting on a computer waiting to come back and haunt us. And don't get me started on those saddos who spend all day crawling through the internet, desperate to use any off-colour remark they can find to cancel someone's career. Get a life ffs.

- Sony Walkman – I didn't actually have one. The only portable tape recorder I owned would've needed two people to lift it. It still chewed up all my tapes though.

- Sweets – fruit salads, cola bottles, blackjacks, spangles, shrimps, sherbet dip dabs (for 40 years I honestly thought they were called 'dib dabs' until I researched the book) and, of course, space dust. I'm well-past 50 now and have a mouth full of crowns & fillings which give me occasional problems but I still wouldn't swap them for a sweet-free adolescence (that may not be entirely true but you know what I mean).

- Top of the Pops (TOTP) – I can't quite believe I didn't use this programme as a topic for a story but it crops up so often that I just spread it over several stories instead. I know I jip it (and rightly so – miming bands, cheesy dancers, irritating/terrifying presenters) but I genuinely loved it. We all did. What else was there to watch on a Thursday evening? That was actually a rhetorical question but I don't mind if you tell me – the Facebook page is still up (under Absolute Very First Time …).

- Toys – I've got a real soft spot for the toys of our youth. Well, more than a soft spot. I've spent hundreds of pounds buying up the original versions on eBay (after my mum either binned mine or sold them for less than a quid at a car boot sale). That said, I've only their word for it that they're original (rather than recent knock-offs from Eastern Europe) and these are sellers with c.73% positive feedback so I can't be entirely sure. The 'toys' that really got on my wick were weebles. Airfix distributed them in the UK which goes to prove they should've stuck to what they knew best (ie making model kits of military hardware with so many fiddly parts that you either lost them or broke them long before you had the opportunity to smear paint and glue all over your parents' dining room table).

- Winnie The Pooh – along with Back to the Future, The Muppets, Rupert the Bear, Blues Brothers and the Royal Wedding, the Poohmeister was a topic I had on my shortlist for future stories. I also had Jackanory, Top Trumps, Evel Knievel, the Goodies, Barbara Woodhouse, The Liver Birds and Anneka Rice's backside on a longer list. Some of these are a shame not to have covered, some deserved no more than a line or two anyway and there are a couple where potential legal repercussions mean I've probably dodged a bullet.

Glossary for Younger Readers

A

Adam Ant - pop star who dressed like a pirate and is now a couple of tracks short of an LP (an LP is a sort of playlist but all by the same artist).

Adverts - short films which made us laugh and want to buy stuff. I'm not sure what the equivalent is nowadays.

Animal House - if you ever go to a toga party (be careful, it's probably cultural appropriation), this film is why.

Atlases - big encyclopedia-like books we used to help us reach our holiday destination. What? I've got to explain encyclopedias too?

B

Banana Splits - not a dessert but a bunch of blokes dressed up like extras in a Star Wars film (and you didn't create the first Star Wars instalment, we did).

Barratts cigarettes - sweets. No really.

Bill Grundy - a dirty fucker according to the Sex Pistols (easy-listening 70s band).

Black & White Minstrels - an imaginary act dreamt up to mess with your heads.

Blobs - weird-flavoured sweets made by Trebor; fat people (name-calling was not only legal but encouraged in our day).

Blockbusters - shop which sold pre-downloaded films; quiz show where asking for a 'p' made the nation wet itself laughing (we were easily amused).

Brooke Bond Tea Cards - like pokemon cards but educational and about real stuff.

Bucks Fizz - Eurovision winners when the UK won it all the time (see also Sandie Shaw, Lulu, Brotherhood of Man).

C

Carry On - movies in the 60s/70s which were allowed to include innuendo without adding trigger warnings about it.

Cash - something we used to buy stuff which invariably led to something else called 'change.' Sort of like 'contactless.'

Cinema tickets - real bits of paper given to us by a real person; mush in the pocket of our jeans after our mum washed them.

Cliff Richard - you don't want to know.

D

Dick Dastardly - the sort of name we gave to our villains so we knew they were the bad guy. You've got a bent copper called 'H' and a TV kingpin called Simon Cowell, neither of which are much help.

Doc Martens - tough bovver boots worn by skinheads to ... what was that? They're worn by teenage girls now? Fair do's.

E

Eurovision - the only current TV show where taking the mickey is still allowed.

F

Findus Crispy Pancakes - nutritious food providing one of your 5-a-day.

Font - I've used a smaller one for this section because you're young and you've got better eyesight than the rest of us.

Freeman Hardy & Willis - a shoe shop not a 70s prog rock band.

G

Goal - something which happened if the ref said it did (without the need for endless replays and an appeals process). See also '**wicket**' and '**try**.'

Goldfish in a bag - what we won at the fair and flushed down the loo later.

Grease - not the country that nearly went bust but a film starring the old bloke who did some dad dancing in Pulp Fiction.

H

Hamble - long before the Weeping Angels turned up on Dr Who, this was the most terrifying thing on kids telly.

Hamlet - a cigar or a play by Shakespeare - neither of which you will have heard of.

Hitchhiking - like Uber but free.

HOW - TV show full of Native American chants which, despite that, was cancelled only when Fred Dinenage said it was.

Hula Hoop - something you'd find in a playground long before it turned up in a gym; tasty snack we were allowed in our school lunchbox in the old days.

Hurty feelings - something we needed to get over rather than report to the police.

I

Indians - red ones who fought cowboys as their squaw (our little sister) watched from the teepee (a sheet over a chair).

Interviews - wide-ranging discussions where celebs and sporting stars gave honest and/or entertaining answers without trying to sell anything or reading a script written for them by a PR Exec.

J

Jackanory - programme telling stories to kids so their parents didn't have to.

Janitor - dodgy old bloke allowed to work in schools without a background check; mild-mannered canine superhero; usual occupation of the baddy who would've got away with it if not for pesky kids.

Jimmy Savile - famous car safety campaigner (see '**seat belts**') who kept telling us about his deviant behaviour but we all thought he was pulling our leg.

John Player - major sports sponsor like Nike; fag brand ... no, really.

Joke - something we avoided filing a complaint about even if we didn't find it funny.

K

Knickerbocker Glory - an ice cream sensation not an act in a porn video.

L

Lectures - stuff we got to see on BBC's Open University (unless the test card was on) rather than when we were naively expecting our TV dramas, films & pop bands to entertain us instead.

Leg Warmers - granny socks which your mum wore when she thought she was young & trendy.

Luton airport - where ladies in adverts came from.

M

Magic Roundabout - like In the Night Garden but with drug references and anti-French propaganda.

Mental health - something we took the piss out of rather than used as an excuse to have our exam marks upgraded.

Mix Tapes - manual Spotify shuffle.

Monty Python - you'd have no comedy to watch if this lot didn't exist (you do still have comedy to watch don't you?)

N

Non-crime hate crime - do you ever imagine things which might be invented when you're older? We did too ... but we sure as hell never guessed this one.

O

Obesity in children - a condition we cleverly managed to avoid by exercising & avoiding double helpings of everything.

Offence - something we routinely gave and took but used to laugh off either way.

Open University - tertiary educational establishment where anyone could join virtual courses without any grade requirement. You just call it 'university' nowadays.

P/Q

Phone boxes - the way we contacted our parents; urinal; advertising hoarding for local prostitutes.

Polaroids - iPhone photos but not as easy to send pictures of genitals to widespread distribution (yes, annoying I know).

Postcards - whatsapp messages which took several weeks to reach their target.

Punch & Judy - puppet show about domestic violence. See also '**Muppets**'.

R

Radio Rentals - shop that rented, er, TVs.

Raleigh Chopper - bike but without the capability to fold into a neat little package you could pop into your satchel.

Record collection - like Spotify but took up half our bedroom floor and repeated the same line when we scratched the vinyl (this is how we invented DJs for you).

Recorder - a musical instrument played at school (see also '**triangle**') - the equivalent of today's bassoon, marimba or Sibelius software system.

Rubiks Cube - like a DS game but much harder and without the same amount of snipers/murderers/aliens/carjackers.

S

Seat belts - optional car accessory.

Shops - places we walked into and paid for stuff in cash (I know - weird, right?)

Smash Hits - a magazine which taught us the lyrics to pop songs when we couldn't google them.

Smiths - the best band of all time. Yes, even better than One Direction.

Smog - what killed us before you lot gave us COVID.

Sodastream - device to make homemade coke or lemonade indistinguishable from the real brands (ask your folks to explain the joke).

Swearing - something which could get us fired, taken off telly or given a criminal record - a bit like defining a woman incorrectly does today.

T

Television - how we watched sport, music and news before iPhones. Too big to fit in your pocket though.

Tony Blackburn - very famous and much-loved TV & radio personality who thought this book was so terrific he begged me to include his quote on the back cover (if I gave him £45 that is).

U

Under-age drinking - allowable by pubs in the 70s/80s without even having to produce a fake ID.

V

Video Nasties - Netflix films which our parents got their tits in a tangle over.

W

Winklepickers - toe-deforming footwear (see also '**pixie boots**' and '**Clarks shoe-sizing machines**').

Woolies/WH Smiths - bricks & mortar versions of Amazon but more expensive. Stocked sweets and porn mags though.

X/Y/Z

Xmas No.1 - something which mattered in our day. Like the winner of the Miss World competition.

Yellow Pages - google but far slower. Used by old farts trying to find their out-of-print book (yes I know, very funny and thanks for the comparison).

Young Ones - comedy show with an unhealthy obsession about ageing pop stars (see also ~~Cliff~~... on second thoughts don't).

These stories show just how much the world has changed since we were young; sometimes for the better (I can't actually think of any examples but I'm trying to sound even-handed – pub opening-hours perhaps?) but often not. Making life 'easier' or 'fairer' or 'safer' or 'more considerate' also tends to suck the joy out of it too.

More than that, it encourages people to take offence where none is intended, buoyed by an establishment which seems to pay far more notice to a handful of loud dissenters on social media than it does the silent, decent majority which recognises that not everything is perfect but muddles along anyway.

Our parents always thought that things were better in 'the good old days' (remember the old music hall show?) so perhaps this is simply the order of things as each generation gets older?

So, no wonder we look back at our childhood years with rose-tinted glasses and unbridled nostalgia for a time when life really did seem far simpler.

Roman Bank
Publishing